Two processes have dominated the development of European society during the 19th and 20th centuries: the growth of industry and the growth of cities. This growth has been accompanied by dramatic changes in people's life style. As living standards have improved, people have come to expect a higher quality of urban environment. What was acceptable 25 years ago is rarely so now.

For some of us, the modern urban environment is dynamic and stimulating; for others it is hectic and wearing. Whatever our feelings about it, the quality of that environment is an issue of keen interest to us all. It is therefore timely that the Council of Europe should sponsor an initiative—the European Campaign for Urban Renaissance—aimed at promoting 'a better life in towns'.

The intention behind the campaign is to build out from the ideas generated by European Architectural Heritage Year, which proved such a success in stimulating public awareness in the conservation of historically and architecturally important places and buildings. The new campaign, however, is planned to embrace the much wider theme of urban renewal and the improvement of urban living, and is aimed principally at exchanging experience between the countries of the Council of Europe. As a means of doing this, the campaign will focus on five issues: improving urban environmental quality; rehabilitating areas of older buildings; providing social, cultural and economic opportunities; achieving community development and participation; and illustrating the role of local authorities.

As the host country for the launching of the campaign, we have taken the opportunity of having this report prepared on our post-war experience of urban change. In it the author discusses the lessons that have been learned, and some of the issues likely to be facing us in the future. The questions raised will not be unfamiliar elsewhere in Europe, though the different circumstances of other countries may well produce different interpretations and solutions.

In the United Kingdom, we have done much since 1945 to improve the quality of life in our towns and cities. Perhaps the most obvious of the many substantial improvements achieved are in people's housing conditions and standards of health. Most of our slums have been replaced, a great deal of old housing stock has been rehabilitated and air and water pollution controls have brought a marked improvement in public health and the general environment. For all the success, the road forward has not always been a smooth one. Here and there, policies designed to solve old problems have created problems of their own. Who, for example, could foresee the adverse effects that later arose from policies—very necessary at the time—to encourage the movement of people and jobs away from congested metropolitan areas? Or from the large-scale clearance and redevelopment programmes of the 1950s and 1960s?

The lessons learnt from the impact of former urban policies have not been lost on us in our present thinking. Today we seek to guide urban change in a sensitive fashion: economical in the use of resources, causing the least possible disruption to communities, and giving every scope for public involvement. In the United Kingdom we are encouraging the ordinary citizen to play a role in improving his own environment. In essence we are endeavouring to create a climate within which people have as much control as possible over their environment.

If the campaign is to bring a true renaissance in the quality of urban living, we need to remember that cities and towns are not simply buildings and spaces. They are essentially places where people live, work and play. And the best safeguard of the quality of life in towns and cities is to have caring, informed and involved local citizens.

The Rt. Hon. Tom King, MP,
Minister for Local Government
and Environmental Services

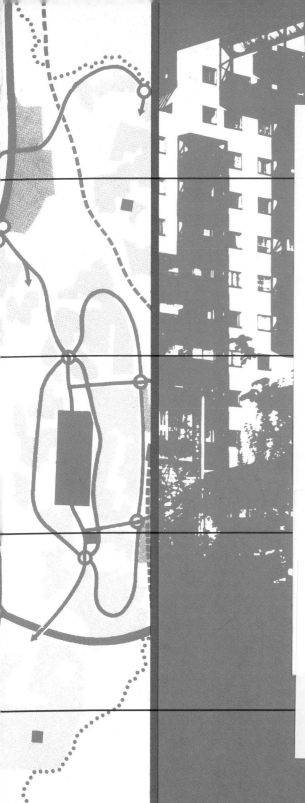

Urban renaissance

A better life in towns

Environment,
London 1980

Acknowledgments

Thanks are due to the following individuals and organisations for supplying photographs: Aerofilms and Aero Pictorial Ltd; Architectural Press; Peter Baker Photography; City Engineer, Birmingham; Bovis Homes Ltd; British Leyland British Railways Board; Metropolitan Borough of Calderdale; Camera Press; Central Press; Civic Trust; Coventry City Council; Cumbernauld Development Corporation; Darlington Evening Despatch; Docklands Development Organisation; John Donat; Dowsett Engineering Ltd; Durham City Council; Fox Photos; The Glasgow Herald and Evening Times; Henry Grant, AIIP; Greater Glasgow Passenger Transport Executive; Greater London Council; Greater Manchester County Council; Guardian Newspapers Ltd; Hanover Housing Association; Rod Hackney; Robb and Campbell Harper Studios Ltd; Geoffrey Holland; Inter-Action Trust Ltd; Ironbridge Gorge Museum Trust; Kentish Times; London News Association; London Transport Museum; Mansell Collection; Merseyside County Museums; Mary Mitchell, FLI, FFB; City Engineer, Newcastle; Oxford City Council; Press Association; Michael Reid; Runcorn Development Corporation; Sheffield City Libraries; Henk Snoek; Stanland; Syndication International; Tyne and Wear Transport; University College of Swansea and Swansea City Council; Swansea Museum; Welwyn Garden City Development Corporation; Westminster City Council.

ISBN 0 11 751489 6

Prepared by the Department of the Environment and the Central Office of Information.
First published 1980

Printed in England for Her Majesty's Stationery Office by Robert Stockwell Ltd.
Dd 8203869 Pro 14280

Contents

Illustrations

Introduction

A campaign for urban renaissance has particular significance and relevance for the United Kingdom. Having been one of the first countries to experience rapid industrialisation and rapid urbanisation, we now appear to be in the vanguard in experiencing the problems of arresting the decline of our large cities and combating a growing disillusionment with the quality of urban life.

The United Kingdom has long been one of the most highly urbanised countries in the world. During the 19th century its population increased nearly four-fold, and it had reached 39 million people by the dawn of the 20th century. By then over six out of every 10 people were living in towns and cities. Now, 80 years later, the population has increased by a further 50 per cent and reached 56 million. Today over three out of every four people live in towns.

During the 19th century the United Kingdom was transformed from an agricultural and commercial country into a highly industrialised and urbanised nation. London's population grew from 1 million to 6.5 million. Outside London population growth was concentrated in the North of England, in South Wales, in the central lowlands of Scotland and in Northern Ireland, reflecting the growth of new industries— coal, iron and steel, shipbuilding and textiles —in those areas. These industries clamoured for labour. Towns sprang up in new and often unsuitable locations, where people could live within walking distance of work. Row upon row of small, drab two-storey houses, often back to back, huddling close to the factory, coal mine or works, an atmosphere polluted by smoke and noise, and a landscape polluted by spoil heaps—these became all too familiar components of the 19th century industrial and urban scene.

Yet the century was not one of unrelieved urban and environmental squalor. The medieval towns outside the new industrial areas retained and enhanced their charm and and character, since the new urban areas had not been grafted on to the pre-industrial, basically agrarian pattern of development. (These towns were to come more under threat in the 20th century.) The Victorians recognised the need for pure water supply, good drainage, street lighting and pavements as essential basic services for urban living, and developed public health legislation which enabled local authorities to control at least the sanitary conditions in towns. They also recognised the need for urban open spaces, and their public parks are still a valued feature

in the urban scene. Furthermore, some enlightened industrialists created communities for their employees which foreshadowed uncannily the 'new town' concept which was not to come to full fruition until after World War II.

Even so, the Industrial Revolution, as it unfolded during the 19th century, bequeathed massive problems of poor housing, drab environments, and urban dereliction. It has taken most of this century, interrupted by two world wars, to eradicate its worst excesses. The task is still far from complete.

The 20th century has produced its own, different, problems and legacies. As electricity and oil supplanted steam power, as new and diverse industries grew untrammelled by the need to be near sources of raw materials, and as roads undermined the monopoly of the railways, the economic centre of gravity of the nation moved to the South-East and the Midlands. Today one out of every three people in the United Kingdom live in London and the South-East of England. This region alone has a population of nearly 17 million, which is greater than the total populations of 15 out of the 21 member states of the Council of Europe.

This structural economic imbalance would have been even greater but for the strenuous efforts of all post-war Governments to encourage new industry, through the provision of financial and other incentives to go to areas where the older basic industries are declining; through the renewal of outworn Victorian environments and improvement of their communication links with the rest of the country; and through firm control over new development in the South-East. But it remains a fundamental structural problem underlying many of Britain's urban planning policies. The problem is likely to become still more complex as the economic and social implications of the microprocessor revolution, as yet only dimly foreseen, unfold.

The 20th century has also been the age of the motor vehicle— a potent instrument for the dispersal of people from the large cities. At first people moved out from the inner areas to the periphery, creating the explosion of suburbia which was so marked in the inter-war years. Since the war, car ownership has increased six-fold and people have moved out beyond the green belts encircling the conurbations and larger cities, to the towns and villages beyond. Although Greater

An urban land

Population growth

1751	1871	1978	2001
10.9 million	27.4 million	55.8 million	58.0 million (projection)

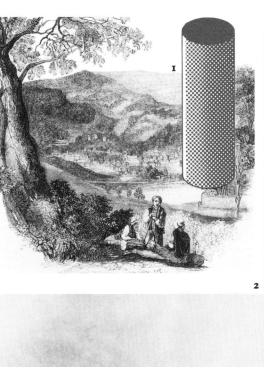

Britain's Industrial Revolution brought with it massive population growth and rapid urbanisation. During the 19th century, the country's population grew nearly four-fold, to 39 million, and became increasingly concentrated in the towns. Today there are 56 million people in Britain and over 75 per cent of them live in towns. Nearly one third are concentrated in London and the South-East. It is massive changes such as these which have brought about the need for urban planning in the developed countries. As one of the earliest industrialised nations, Britain was one of the first to experience the problems caused by rapid urbanisation, and it is now among the first to face the problems of a post-industrial era.

The changing face of urban Britain: Sheffield seen from the same vantage point, 1, in pre-industrial times, 2, in the 19th century and 3, today.

London continued to grow throughout the first half of the century, reaching over 8 million people, some of the inner areas have been losing population since before World War I. In the last two decades the outer areas have also been losing people and the population of the conurbation has declined to just under 7 million. This exodus of over 1 million people is a net·figure. It masks quite substantial inflows into the metropolis outweighed by even larger outflows. The effects have been felt throughout the South-East and intensified development pressures already created by indigenous population growth. The same picture emerges in the other conurbations and large cities, which are all losing population at varying rates. In fact the total population of all the conurbations—Greater London, West Midlands, Manchester, Merseyside, West Yorkshire, Tyneside and Glasgow—has declined by over 5 per cent in the last 20 years.

It says much for British town and country planning legislation that this exodus has been handled in a way which has avoided creating an urban film over the countryside at large. For 30 years it has been firm policy to refuse permission for the building of single houses in the countryside— the individual's dream when wishing to escape from the increasing noise and discomfort of urban living. This exodus, plus a post-war population growth of over 5 million, has been largely contained within and around the existing urban fabric either through planned dispersal to new towns or controlled expansion of existing towns. People may bemoan the loss of agricultural land for development on the periphery of towns, but it is still possible to travel the length of the land and see a countryside undefiled by sporadic development.

This exodus, partly encouraged and planned in the post-war years, has reflected a growing disillusionment with the quality of urban life in the conurbations and large cities. Its effect has been to compound the urban problems bequeathed from the last century, especially in the inner areas of cities. These are now characterised by substantial areas of decay, outworn environment, lack of employment, and the prevalence of poverty and other social problems, and have become the focus for concerted action designed to improve and rehabilitate them.

This century, and particularly the post-war period, has seen urban traffic congestion emerge as a major issue, posing a serious threat to the urban environment—not least in the historic or 'heritage' towns such as Bath, Chester and York. Pollution from traffic noise and traffic fumes, the impact of traffic and all its regulatory paraphernalia on the visual environment, and the prospect of ever more urban road building to accommodate ever growing volumes of traffic, have stimulated much interest in the quality of the urban environment. In the last ten years the conservation of our urban heritage has become a dominant theme, and its scope has widened from the preservation of individual buildings of historic or architectural interest to the conservation of whole areas within towns or even of a whole town or village. Interest in conservation has been further stimulated by the Council of Europe's European Architectural Heritage year, which was launched in 1975.

The United Kingdom's urban problems are varied, deep-seated and complex. This report, chronicling British urban planning policies since the war, their successes and failures, some of the lessons learnt and some of the difficulties which will face us for the rest of the century, may therefore be of some interest and relevance to other nations grappling with similar problems.

This Report is chiefly structured around the five themes identified for the Urban Renaissance campaign—the quality of the urban environment; rehabilitating older residential areas; providing social and economic infrastructures; achieving community participation; and the role of the local authorities.

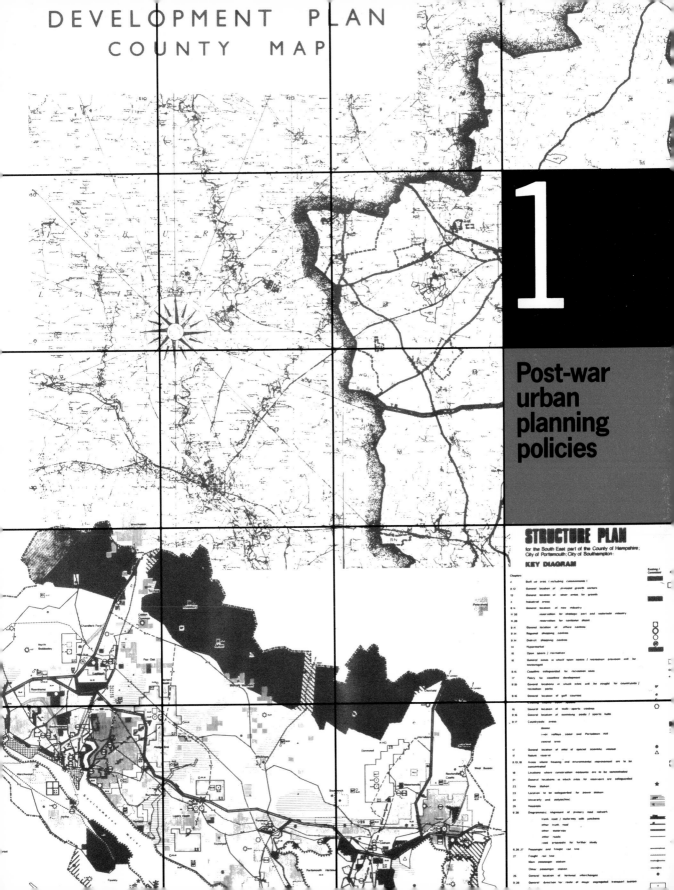

DEVELOPMENT PLAN
COUNTY MAP

1

Post-war urban planning policies

This chapter deals with the broad thrust of British urban planning policies since World War II. During this period these policies, responding to changes in public attitudes, have traversed the whole gamut of urban renewal—using the term in its widest sense to cover conservation and rehabilitation as well as redevelopment of urban areas.

Comprehensive reconstruction of cities—slum clearance, redevelopment of city centres and much urban road building—coupled with policies of encouraging the dispersal of people and jobs from the large conurbations, has gradually given way to comprehensive conservation and rehabilitation of our urban fabric, with attention focussed on the problems of decaying inner city areas. Regulative planning has given way to indicative planning. There is much more emphasis on the need for public participation in the formulation of urban plans and policies and on community involvement in the urban environment. As the consequences of the post-war 'reconstruction era' have emerged there has been a growing realisation that the built environment, the social environment and the economic environment in urban areas form an indivisible whole. The real complexities inherent in stimulating effective urban renewal have become more apparent.

The immediate post-war years

The nation emerged from the war with formidable urban problems. There had been a large-scale redistribution of people through wartime evacuation, much dispersal of industry and much destruction of homes. The population itself had grown by 1.5 million since 1939. Towns already overcrowded faced a further influx of people as demobilisation proceeded and evacuees returned. Industry needed to be redeployed and re-equipped; labour and materials were scarce. All this was added to the massive problems of urban obsolescence inherited from the Industrial Revolution of the previous century.

There was a universal desire to build Britain anew. This was the period of the creation of the Welfare State—the publication of the Beveridge Report, *Social insurance and allied services*, which formed the basis of the post-war National Insurance scheme, and the setting up of the National Health Service. On the urban front there was a remarkable consensus amongst all political parties and shades of public opinion that more housing

was needed desperately, and that people and jobs should be dispersed to new towns to provide room for the reconstruction and remodelling of existing cities; but it was also agreed that those cities should be prevented from spreading into the countryside through strict control over the use and development of all land. Industry was to be stimulated to move to the older declining areas to achieve a better balance throughout the country.

These objectives reflected the problems inherited from the past. Tight control over the use of land was considered essential in a small, densely populated island. The need to control the outward spread of cities reflected concern over inter-war failures to control the spread of suburbia. The concept of building complete new towns with all their facilities and services had roots going back to the 19th century, having been stimulated by Ebenezer Howard's publications on 'garden cities' and their expression in reality in the construction of Letchworth and Welwyn Garden City north of London. The idea of a gracious and spacious urban environment in a rural setting was a natural reaction to congested and ugly Victorian towns. There was a firmly held view that, given a pleasant and decent urban environment, social problems would look after themselves—a form of environmental determinism which appears somewhat simplistic in retrospect. The legacy of outworn housing and drab urban areas inherited from the Industrial Revolution, compounded by war damage, made comprehensive redevelopment, rather than conservation or rehabilitation, a national imperative.

A spate of legislation provided the framework for the execution of these policies. Not surprisingly it had a heavy bias towards State intervention.

A small Ministry of Town and Country Planning was set up in 1943. The Minister was charged with the duty of: 'securing consistency and continuity in the framing and execution of a national policy with respect to the use and development of land throughout England and Wales'. Similar powers were given to Ministers in Scotland and Northern Ireland. (The Ministry of Town and Country Planning later became the Ministry of Housing and Local Government, and, later still, the Department of the Environment, thus providing a focus on urban planning matters within central government throughout the post-war period.)

In 1944, town-planning legislation gave local authorities powers to buy land in war-damaged or obsolete urban areas for comprehensive redevelopment so that post-war reconstruction would not be hampered.

In 1947 an Act of Parliament gave local authorities comprehensive powers to control development generally. All development of land in town and countryside was made the subject of planning permission—the term 'development' being defined very widely in the Act of Parliament. Only minor development and agricultural activities were excluded from the need for planning permission. If the local planning authority refused planning permission, or attached conditions to its approval which were unacceptable to the applicant, he had the right of 'appeal' to the then Minister of Town and Country Planning.

This system of detailed control over development needed a planning framework if decisions on individual cases were not to be arbitrary and piecemeal. This was provided by a 'development plan' for the area concerned. Each planning authority was required to draw up a statutory development plan showing the proposed pattern of land use over the next 20 years, based on a survey of land uses and activities in their area and an analysis of the main changes that could be foreseen. These plans had to be submitted to the Minister for approval and were intended to be reviewed and revised every five years.

Central government took powers in the Distribution of Industry Act of 1945 to secure the proper balance of industry throughout the country by stimulating industry to move to the older declining areas—the 'Development Areas' as they were then called. These powers provided for building factories and improving basic services such as transport, housing and roads.

Central government also took powers in the New Towns Act of 1946 to provide machinery for building new towns. The Minister was empowered to designate sites for new towns and to set up 'development corporations'. These were given wide-ranging powers to acquire any land or property within the designated area and to build houses, offices, factories and other essential buildings, as well as estate roads and, if necessary, the main services for the creation of the town, all in accordance with a master plan which they had prepared and submitted for ministerial approval. There were detailed and sometimes complex administrative arrangements for sharing and co-ordinating

the provision of water, gas, electricity, sewerage and other facilities. These new town development corporations were wholly financed by central government by means of loans repayable over periods agreed with the Treasury, and also received the subsidies payable to local authorities carrying out comparable duties, for example house-building.

All this legislation did not of course solve the pressing post-war problems, but it did provide a comprehensive framework within which solutions could be sought.

Despite the immediate post-war austerities —rationing, the issue of licences for private-sector building, shortages of materials and resources—and despite, too, the obvious difficulties of finding suitable sites which did not take good agricultural land, had good communications and were not too far from, or too near to, the parent conurbation or town, 12 new towns were launched in England and Wales by 1951. At the same time, local authorities were repairing war-damaged houses and building new ones as fast as limited finance and materials permitted. There was no question of starting on slum clearance. Public opinion would not countenance the demolition of any housing when all houses, fit or unfit, temporary or permanent, were urgently needed. Work had started in severely bombed cities such as Coventry, Plymouth, Portsmouth and Southampton.

Even so, there was a growing impatience to see towns and cities reconstructed. In the early 1950s, as the time became ripe to dismantle various rationing and licensing controls, a long-pent-up pressure for redevelopment was unleashed. Redevelopment was to become the dominant aspect in the urban renewal scene for the next 20 years.

The 1950s and 1960s – dispersal and redevelopment

During the 1950s major strides were made in fulfilling the post-war objectives (see page 12). New towns and planned expansions of existing towns catered for the planned dispersal of people and jobs from the cities; green belts and strict development control coped in the main with the much larger unplanned exodus of people from

The garden city concept

In the 20th century there has been a movement away from towns by city-dwellers disillusioned with the quality of urban life. British planners have been concerned to control this flow and prevent indiscriminate development of the countryside.

In the first decades of the century, the 'garden cities' built at Letchworth and Welwyn, north of London, aimed to create a salubrious, semi-rural environment. After World War I, the pressing need for large quantities of new housing led to the building of large suburban estates which, though well built and spacious, often lacked basic amenities, such as shops and recreational facilities.
1, Parkway Close, Welwyn Garden City, in 1930; 2, a housing estate in Cricklewood, North West London, circa 1933.

1

2

Hampstead Garden
Suburb, 3, laid out in the
1930s, was green and
spacious, and well
provided with social
amenities.

The shortcomings of
suburban development
made the garden city
concept seem once more
attractive, and the
widespread need for new
housing after World War II
resulted in the creation of
the first new towns.
The new town centres at
Crawley, 4, Basildon, 5,
and Hemel Hempstead, 6,
illustrate the planners'
priorities for these new
developments: offices, car
parks, shops and
pedestrian precincts, in an
agreeable setting.

3

5

cities. A massive slum clearance programme was launched, widening out to embrace large-scale and comprehensive renewal of the central areas of hundreds of towns, and urban road-building accelerated to cope with mounting traffic problems.

The 'overspill' programme

In the 1950s the inelegantly termed 'overspill' programme—the planned dispersal of people and jobs from the congested conurbations to provide opportunities for the renewal of the inner areas of those conurbations to more spacious standards—was a key feature in urban policies.

Early in the decade the Government of the day passed the Town Development Act of 1952. This enabled conurbations to reach agreements with other local authorities under which they would jointly provide houses and where necessary new factories to take overspill population. Central government made grants on services and housing but otherwise it was left to the local authorities to make whatever arrangements they considered appropriate. By the end of the 1960s there were over 30 of these schemes, involving six conurbations.

In the 1950s the first generation of new towns began to get into their stride. The larger ones around London were being planned for an ultimate population of 60–80,000—considered at that time to be the optimum size for a self-contained town. They were translating into reality the town-planning concepts of the time. These early new towns were designed around the basic urban unit of the neighbourhood—a residential area containing about 6–10,000 people with its own shopping, schools and other services and with industrial estates carefully segregated from housing. Experiments were being made, not without some misgivings, in designing traffic-free shopping areas in town centres.

There were of course problems. There was the 'battlefield' effect of large-scale constructional activity. There were phasing difficulties as houses and factories appeared ahead of shopping and other community facilities. And there were the human problems, for the development corporations, of absorbing a daily influx of new families coming into unfamiliar surroundings. Moreover it was the younger people who were moving out of the crowded cities, bringing their young children with them and thus placing a heavy burden on the authorities,

who had quickly to provide sufficient school places in primary and secondary schools. Parents and grandparents tended to stay behind in the large cities and the age structure of the population in the new towns became unbalanced. Social problems were created as families were split. It became necessary to relax the strict policy that housing would be available to people moving to the new towns only if they had a job there. Despite these pioneering difficulties the new towns flourished, and by the end of the 1950s they were not only proving a successful experiment in urban design but also showing that they would be profitable, as corporations began to repay the loans to central government from the revenues created.

New towns and town expansion schemes were linked with the planned dispersal of people and jobs from the conurbations. But there was a far larger unplanned and voluntary exodus of people from the larger cities which was putting pressure on the peripheries of towns and threatening to extend the inter-war suburban sprawl into the countryside. For every one person moving to new or expanded towns there were over four moving out voluntarily to other areas. This exodus was kept under control through the operation of the new planning legislation strongly reinforced by the introduction of 'green belts' around all the large cities.

Green belts

The green belt concept was not new. Queen Elizabeth 1 in 1580 and James 1 less than half a century later had tried unsuccessfully to put a green belt around London. In the 1930s the London County Council pioneered a green belt around the Metropolis and this, incorporated into statutory development plans, has been successful in stopping London's outward sprawl.

In 1955, as the overspill and slum clearance programmes were gaining momentum, the then Minister of Housing and Local Government recommended that green belts should be established to check the further growth of large built-up areas, to prevent neighbouring towns from merging into one another and to preserve the special character of a town. The local planning authorities were invited to submit proposals to be incorporated into their development plans. Within green belts there was to be a permanent and severe restriction on all new building, and on employment which might create pressures for new building.

In the following years green belts were established around all the conurbations and around many historic towns such as Oxford, Cambridge, Bath and York. The concept attracted widespread and deep-rooted public support, and it remains a potent element in shaping the pattern of urban development to the present day. Proposals to adjust the inner boundaries of approved green belts or to allow sizeable development within them never fail to excite lively controversy.

New towns, town expansion schemes, green belts and the development control system instituted in the 1947 Town and Country Planning Act all combined to ensure the successful execution of the dispersal policy without widespread encroachment into the countryside, an achievement now taken for granted and generally undervalued. But if the dispersal policy was a success, the complementary policies for the renewal of existing towns were less successful and created problems which are still being unravelled today.

Slum clearance

By 1954 public opinion was ready to accept a major drive on the clearance of slum housing which disfigured hundreds of acres in the inner areas of all the large cities—London, Manchester, Liverpool, Birmingham, and Glasgow and substantial areas in most of the other towns. The new housing and slum clearance programmes were vigorously sustained for the rest of the decade. By 1962 some 4.25 million new houses had been built, and nearly 500,000 slum houses cleared. The basic policy was clear-cut—to erase the slums entirely and completely rebuild large areas of the urban fabric to modern standards.

There was no prospect of rehousing the same number of people in these areas after redevelopment. Not only was the slum housing patently unfit—decaying physically and lacking essential facilities such as bathrooms and indoor water closets—it had also been built to very high densities. The slum areas were seriously overcrowded and the houses themselves were over-occupied. Thus the dispersal programme was intended to provide the necessary 'elbow-room' for proper comprehensive redevelopment.

This 'clear felling' policy has subsequently been much criticised because of the social disruption which it created. But it would not have been sustained for over 10 years if it had

not received broad public support. Many people were willing to move out. They had already experienced upheaval during the war and evacuation from the large cities. Families were getting smaller and people were ready to move to a new or expanded town if this meant a new house and employment that much more quickly. There was still a shortage of houses. As late as 1959 the Ministry of Housing and Local Government was still concerned that over 150,000 people were living in some 60,000 caravans as temporary homes. One might more justifiably criticise the predominance of high-rise blocks of flats in the developments which were emerging on the cleared areas, and the fact that these areas were to become the domain of local authorities, thus restricting the choice of housing available to future generations.

Several factors conspired to favour 'high-density, high-rise' schemes in the redevelopment areas. There was strong pressure to prevent further urban sprawl, which found expression in the green belt policy. This had a clear implication that there should be higher densities, albeit governed by modern standards of adequate open space, within the cities. There had been some criticisms that the new towns on green-field sites were 'wasting' land within their designated areas by building at too low a density. This general feeling that redevelopment ought to be at a high density reinforced the views of the local authorities, who naturally wanted to rehouse as many people as possible in the cleared slum areas. High blocks were in tune with the architectural fashion of the day. And this was further reinforced by a government system of housing subsidies to local authorities which encouraged tall buildings.

Eventually, there was a public reaction to the social, environmental and visual consequences of this form of urban renewal which was sufficiently strong to result in a major change of direction in urban planning policies.

Town centre redevelopment

As the economy prospered and shortages of materials lessened, the post-war reconstruction process widened to embrace comprehensive redevelopment of the central areas of most towns and cities. Changes in retail patterns—the appearance of supermarkets—and the growth of service

'Big is beautiful'

At the end of World War II, the reconstruction of Britain's overcrowded and war-damaged city centres was a vital necessity. In the 1950s the planned dispersal of people and jobs from the cities enabled large areas of urban slums to be demolished and replaced with comprehensive new housing schemes. High-rise blocks met the demand for high population densities. They also matched the architectural fashions of the day, and it was not until the late 1960s that their social and aesthetic

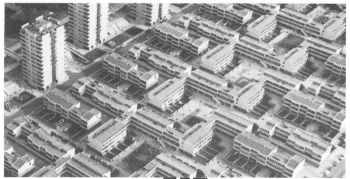

shortcomings caused a public reaction against them.
1, The Pepys Estate, Lewisham, London; 2, the Doddington Road Estate, Battersea, London; 3, the Millpool Estate, Birmingham. Thamesmead, 4, on the south bank of the Thames, is London's biggest and most recent housing development, built between 1965 and 1980 and providing accommodation for 60,000 people.

The new trend in housing development was matched by large commercial schemes combining offices, shops and supermarkets. 5, One of Britain's best known commercial developments, the Bull Ring Centre in Birmingham.

3

5

1

2

4

7

8

6

The creation of entire new towns as a means of relieving pressure on existing cities was the logical conclusion of post-war policies of comprehensive redevelopment. Since the late 1940s, 21 new towns have been designated in England, two in Wales and five in Scotland, their target populations ranging from 30,000 to nearly 300,000. Their object has generally been the same—to provide a planned combination of housing, employment and social and recreational facilities and attract people of all income levels and social and professional groups. Harlow, 25 miles north of London, was designated as a new town in 1947, and has now almost reached its target population of 90,000. The master plan, 6, drawn up before building began in 1949 made skilful use of the existing landscape, and an aerial view, 7, reveals the large number of trees and open spaces.
8, Glenrothes, 30 miles north of Edinburgh, was designated as a new town in 1948 and has a target population of 70,000.

industries, particularly office employment, were creating strong pressures for redevelopment.

The spirit of the time was expressed in a conference on the rebuilding of city centres held in 1960 by the Civic Trust, at which it was strongly argued that unique opportunities would be lost if the piecemeal development of city centres were allowed to continue. The danger was foreseen that the most important areas of countless towns all over the country would be rebuilt without any coherent theme and the existing street pattern, increasingly outmoded by the mounting volume of traffic, would be frozen for another half century. Comprehensive renewal was advocated through unified land assembly carried out by local authorities, and with whole areas being redesigned as an architectural whole. By 1962 nearly 400 town centre redevelopment schemes were being planned or executed, transforming city centres with new shopping, large offices and new roads. There were increasingly complex arrangements between local authorities and developers whereby the former purchased the land, the latter developed it, and both parties shared in the resulting revenues.

By the early 1960s the sheer scale and pace of urban renewal was creating problems. Demand was beginning to outstrip capacity in the construction industry and building costs were rising sharply. There was a shortage of land for new housing. Land allocations in the development plans, which were supposed to be sufficient for 20 years, had been used up in less than half that time. Shortages of bricks and other materials had fostered a keen interest in 'industrialised building' techniques—factory-built kits for the rapid building of housing, schools and offices.

The spectre of population growth

This urban reconstruction would probably have slowed down in the mid-1960s but for the twin spectres of a prospective massive population increase and the growth of urban traffic, which provided a powerful boost to continued building. In the 1940s population projections had indicated a fairly static population. The first round of development plans had been prepared on that basis. But the population continued to grow rapidly. It rose from 45 million in 1945 to 50 million by 1951 and to 55 million by 1964. By the early

1960s all the population projections were indicating a continuing increase. There was the possibility that the population might increase to 70–80 million by the end of the century. (In fact, with falling birth rates since the mid-1960s the latest projections indicate a stable population of about 57 million by AD 2000.)

The prospect of population increases of this magnitude added renewed urgency to the reconstruction processes. One result was that a new generation of new towns were being planned with target populations of well over 100,000. Some were being planned on a city scale and there were even tentative ideas of having to build on a conurbation scale in areas like Humberside and Severnside.

The original concept of new towns was also changing. There was less emphasis on the absorption of overspill as their main purpose and more on the concept of 'growth points' within the regional strategies which were beginning to emerge. Several new towns were planned to be grafted on to sizeable existing towns such as Northampton, Peterborough and Warrington. They were to be built in partnership with the existing local authority to provide an impetus for the renewal of the old town and accommodation for the prospective new growth.

Traffic

The growth of urban traffic was the other major factor reinforcing policies aimed at modernising and reshaping urban areas in a comprehensive fashion. In 1951 there were less than 2.5 million private cars in the United Kingdom. Only one family in six had the use of a car. By 1961 the figure had grown to 6 million. Not only did people do more travelling but most of it was done by private car. The sprawling, low-density suburbs built between the wars were not easily served by public transport. Commuting to work was further encouraged by the town-planning practice of insisting that an adequate number of parking places should be provided in each office or commercial building to avoid parking on the streets. This had led to the provision of fairly generous privately controlled parking in city centres.

Traffic congestion had become a major urban problem. In London 1 million people were travelling daily into and out of the central area. Public transport, rail, underground and buses carried 90 per cent of these commuters but the remaining 10 per cent accounted for 100,000 private cars which created morning and evening rush-hour peaks of steadily lengthening duration. All the other large towns and cities were experiencing similar problems. Although the scale of commuting was smaller than in London they were less well served by public transport, so that a much higher proportion of people were travelling to work by car.

Against this background the car ownership projections in the early 1960s were indicating a large and sustained increase in the growth of traffic, with car ownership doubling by 1970 and trebling by 1980. How to cope with the traffic already on the roads and with these huge prospective increases was the daunting problem facing urban transport and town planners.

The Buchanan report

A study of the long-term problems of traffic in towns was carried out by Sir Colin Buchanan, and his report *Traffic in towns* was published in 1963. It was to have a decisive influence on urban transportation planning not only in the United Kingdom but throughout the world.

The report wrestled with the basic dilemma of how to provide a satisfactory balance between efficient traffic movement and civilised urban life. It advocated two main concepts—primary road networks to cater for the main, longer traffic flows in urban areas where traffic would have precedence, and environmental areas (commercial, industrial and residential) where traffic should be subordinated to the needs of those living and working in them. Taking account of the imminent increase in the growth of traffic which was then being forecast, the report emphasised the need to make the fullest use of existing road systems through comprehensive parking and traffic management policies whilst longer-term integrated land-use and transport plans were being prepared and implemented.

A new development plan system

Simultaneously the whole development plan system was under review. The development control system set up in the 1947 Act had stood the test of time, but the development plan system had failed to do so. It had fallen behind the pace of events. There were

lengthy delays in the approval of plans by central government as procedures became more complex. The plans did not reflect the latest projections forecasting massive growth in population and traffic. A new streamlined and decentralised system was instituted. The old development plans, with their precise land allocations, were to be replaced by 'structure plans' prepared by the county councils, which would concentrate on strategic policies for housing, employment, transportation, etc., eschewing the detail of the old plans. The aim was to provide a more flexible and continuous form of guidance for development; central government would be concerned only with the approval of broad strategic issues and not with the host of local detail which the old-style plans had involved. The new-style structure plans were to be underpinned with 'local plans' intended to provide the more specific basis necessary for detailed development control. These plans did not require ministerial approval—a significant departure from the centralised approval system instituted in the 1947 Act. Given this decentralisation, emphasis was laid on the need for full publicity, consultation and public participation in the formulation of proposals before they were approved locally.

'Big is beautiful'

The prevailing ethos of the late 1960s was that 'big is beautiful'. Industries were merging and rationalising in the interests of economy of scale; supermarkets were becoming hypermarkets; plans were afoot to create jumbo-sized government departments; the possibility of reorganising local government into much fewer but very large 'all-purpose' local authorities was being debated vigorously; and new towns, to take only one example, were being conceived on a city or even conurbation scale.

The expectations of the time were succinctly expressed in a 1965 report on the new-style development plans which said: 'We must expect fast-growing population, with higher expectations demanding higher standards, more mobility both in daily life and recreation. This will mean a surge of physical development on a scale that this country has not previously seen and this will occur overwhelmingly in and around the towns . . . '

The concept of 'comprehensiveness' apparently reigned supreme. There were to be comprehensive regional studies, comprehensive land-use and transportation plans and comprehensive reshaping of urban areas. This approach probably reached its apogee in the ambitious plans published in the mid-1960s for the comprehensive redevelopment of Whitehall. These involved sweeping away most of the existing buildings there, with traffic flows put largely underground to enable Parliament Square to be partially pedestrianised.

But the 'swinging sixties' were a turbulent decade, with student unrest in university campuses throughout the world. The post-war consensus on town-planning objectives vanished. Plans to build very large new towns to city scale and ambitious plans to modernise and reshape existing towns were destined not to materialise. Inflation was rising; there were increasing restraints on public expenditure. Public disquiet mounted over the quality of the new development and over the social disruption created by the scale and pace of slum clearance and comprehensive redevelopment. There was an upsurge of interest in conservation and in the general quality of urban life, and a demand for more participation in town-planning policies and processes. The keynotes of the 1970s were to be conservation, rehabilitation and the problems of the inner city areas.

The 1970s – conservation and inner areas

Housing

Housing problems, and the solutions adopted to cope with them, have always been a major element in the totality of urban planning policies. By the end of the 1960s, the emphasis in housing policies was shifting from slum clearance to house improvement. Housing was no longer a matter of urgent national importance as it had been in the post-war period. The problem had become local rather than national, with areas of intense housing stress still remaining in the conurbations and larger cities and new problems of obsolescence and disrepair emerging as more detailed information became available on the condition of the national housing stock.

Chapter 3 deals in more detail with housing renewal policies. In this context it need only be said that house improvement had played only a minor role in housing policy until the mid-1960s. Thereafter, as the national housing programme declined, as criticisms developed about the effects of wholesale slum clearance, and as rising building costs began to make improvement rather than clearance economically desirable, the emphasis in housing policy shifted to comprehensive improvement on an area basis, and to the gradual renewal of residential areas.

In 1969 a Housing Act was passed which widened the scope of house improvement grants (first introduced 20 years earlier in the 1949 Housing Act) and gave local housing authorities new discretionary powers to declare 'general improvement areas' (GIAs). The aim was to improve both housing and the environment in areas capable of providing good living accommodation for many years ahead.

In 1974 a Housing Act introduced the concept of 'housing action areas' (HAAs) designed to give priority to the improvement of areas where poor housing was combined with social stress and deprivation—revealed in a high proportion of households with special problems such as the elderly, single-parent families, the unemployed and the low paid.

The early 1970s saw the discarding of many past assumptions—that run-down housing areas not already in the slum clearance programme were suitable only for demolition and redevelopment and to rehabilitate them would be simply postponing inevitable clearance; that residents of privately rented dwellings in those areas would be content to change their tenancy for a council house or flat; and that the blighting effects of clearance and the dispersal of communities would be outweighed by the benefits of improved housing standards. These attitudes were replaced with policies that advocated a wider, more comprehensive approach focussing on the concept of 'gradual renewal'. This was defined in a ministry circular in 1975 as: '. . . a continuous process of minor rebuilding and renovation which sustains and reinforces the vitality of a neighbourhood in ways responsive to social and physical needs as they develop and change'.

The conservation movement

In the wider urban scene there was a major shift in public opinion, in favour of conservation rather than redevelopment.

The conservation movement had been gathering momentum throughout the 1960s. Indeed as early as 1957 concern was being expressed about slum clearance sweeping away houses of charm and interest. By the mid-1960s the scale and pace of reconstruction and the remorseless growth of urban traffic were leading to anxieties about their environmental effects, particularly on the older historic towns. In 1968 four major conservation studies were launched, in Bath, Chester, Chichester and York.

Although some of the conservation organisations are of long standing—bodies such as the Society for the Protection of Ancient Buildings and the National Trust were established in the 19th century—over 80 per cent of the local amenity societies now in existence have been formed since the mid-1950s. This interest in the urban environment was fostered not only by anxieties over the pace of urban reconstruction but also by a growing disillusionment with the quality of the new development. It was further stimulated by the growth of global interest in environmental pollution in all its forms.

The 1947 Planning Act provided for the preservation of individual buildings of special architectural and historic interest. They could be included in lists compiled by central government for each local authority area. The aim was to ensure that, before any 'listed' building could be demolished or altered in such a way as to affect its character, careful consideration was given to its historic, architectural or other value. Interest in 'facelift' schemes initiated by the Civic Trust and widening public interest in the urban environment led to pressure to conserve not only individual buildings but whole areas judged to be of townscape value either historically or architecturally. In 1967 the passing of the Civic Amenities Act gave local planning authorities power to designate 'conservation areas' with the minimum of procedural complexities, and further legislation extended their control over demolition to all buildings in these areas. There are now over 4,000 conservation areas in population centres ranging from large cities to rural villages within which there is a strong presumption against redevelopment.

The anti-road movement

Another major shift of public opinion occurred in attitudes towards urban roads. In the late 1960s a widespread revulsion grew up against the disruptive effects of large-scale urban road building. The destruction of property involved created opposition under the emotive slogan of 'homes before roads'. The impact of traffic noise on nearby properties led to bitter complaints. Rising costs were criticised and the necessity for new roads challenged when it seemed that they brought little noticeable relief to traffic congestion and that traffic volumes merely increased to fill the new roads to capacity.

In response, the Government investigated ways in which new urban roads could be designed so as to reduce their environmental effects of noise, visual damage and severance of communities, and initiated changes in compensation. Legislation was introduced requiring highway authorities to soundproof houses near to new and improved roads and to pay compensation to householders who were injuriously affected. The earlier specific grant towards the cost of improving and constructing roads was replaced by a single comprehensive transport grant which gave local authorities greater freedom to decide how their transport system, including roads, should be developed.

So just as housing policies have swung from slum clearance to house improvement and the gradual renewal of residential areas, and just as urban reconstruction and redevelopment have given place to urban conservation, so urban transport policies have swung away from the major construction of new roads, which is costly and damaging to the environment, towards small-scale, incremental improvements of the existing road network. The emphasis is now on schemes designed to free central areas from traffic altogether; on bypasses around towns to take through traffic away from them; and on traffic-management measures designed to make the most of existing infrastructure.

The inner city areas

Attention has increasingly focussed on the complex problems of the 'inner cities'—those old areas adjacent to the business and shopping centres. They are often, though not invariably, characterised by a pervasive sense of environmental, economic and social decay. Housing which escaped slum clearance and redevelopment is often of poor quality and set in a drab environment. Reconstruction has lagged behind the bulldozer. There is under-used land; sites and buildings are neglected, and shops boarded up.

The swing to conservation

The general reaction against massive redevelopment at the end of the 1960s was matched by a growing awareness of the need to protect the historic fabric of Britain's towns. Historic town centres were threatened by the growth of urban traffic, and surrounding inner areas could easily slide into dereliction. Even where historic buildings had been recognised as worth preserving, their impact could be spoiled by the scale of adjacent developments.

1, A heavy lorry fills a village street in St Columb Minor, Cornwall.
2, York City centre with the towers of York Minster in the background;
3, urban dereliction, exacerbated by the motor car, in Bath;
4,5, Conservation in the shadow of redevelopment at Guy's Hospital and St James's Gardens, London.

In these areas, economic decline is evident. Factories and firms have moved out taking their skilled workers with them. Some firms have simply died; others, often the small units, have been swept away in the redevelopment processes. There is a mis-match between jobs and skills. The inner areas have a disproportionate amount of semi-skilled and unskilled labour and a disproportionate amount of unemployment.

Social problems abound. These are areas often dominated by publicly subsidised housing with an ever-decreasing amount of privately rented accommodation. Low earning power can deny residents the opportunity of getting a mortgage for house purchase elsewhere so they are 'locked into' the area, where the houses may not command mortgages. These areas are the refuge for the most vulnerable members of society—the homeless and those with personal problems needing social help and support. They are also the traditional home for ethnic minorities, although not exclusively so. Given this degree of environmental and social stress it is not surprising if the inhabitants feel a sense of neglect and powerlessness, and equally not surprising if vandalism and crime increase. Poverty and deprivation are not of course unique to the inner areas of large cities; but these inner areas have more than their fair share.

Concern over these areas arose in many different quarters in the mid-1960s. The then Ministry of Housing and Local Government were at that time carrying out studies of urban renewal policies best suited for the so-called 'twilight areas'. A report on primary schools was advocating educational priority areas designed to concentrate extra resources on deprived communities. Another report called for the unification of social services and the deployment of extra funds in areas of special need, and in particular stressed the need to pay special attention to the housing problems of the elderly, the physically handicapped, one-parent families and large families.

In 1964 a Government Urban Aid programme was launched to help communities in 'areas of special need'. Local authorities were given some limited finance to help them provide local projects such as play schemes, nursery schools, advice centres and language classes for immigrants. In the early 1970s three comprehensive and detailed studies of the problems in the inner areas of large cities were carried out in Liverpool, the London borough of Lambeth, and Birmingham. These studies revealed the full complexity and wide range of problems posed by these inner areas. They also revealed how the mix of problems varied from area to area. Following a Government White Paper, *Policy for the inner cities,* published in 1977, the Inner Urban Areas Act was passed in 1978.

Today there is a firm government commitment, transcending political parties, to tackle the problems in the inner areas. In seven areas special 'partnership' arrangements have been set up to co-ordinate and develop schemes to revitalise inner areas through the joint action of the Government, the local authorities and health authorities and voluntary and community groups. These partnership areas are in Birmingham, Liverpool, Manchester/Salford, Newcastle/Gateshead and in the Lambeth, Hackney-Islington and Dockland areas in London. There are in addition 15 other local authorities where action is co-ordinated and concentrated. Similar arrangements, pre-dating the English partnerships, apply in the case of the Glasgow Eastern Area Renewal project (GEAR). In Northern Ireland, also, arrangements for co-ordinating activities operate in respect of Belfast, which faces serious inner city problems.

All these authorities have prepared comprehensive local strategies for the regeneration of their inner areas based on an analysis of local needs and priorities. The 1978 Act has given them additional powers to designate 'industrial improvement areas' (IIAs) and provide financial assistance to industries in an attempt to stimulate industrial regeneration and the creation of jobs in these areas. Additional resources have been provided by central government for inner areas. In addition an 'inner area dimension' has been given to other national expenditure programmes such as housing, roads, education, health and environmental services, with the aim of concentrating resources on the complex problems involved.

The aim is to create a climate in which returning prosperity will attract people and investment back to these areas. The emphasis is on local self-help and co-ordination of the mutual interests of all local community bodies—employers, trade unions, voluntary bodies and local authorities.

But there are two areas of extensive urban dereliction—the dockland areas in London and Merseyside—which require a different approach. Here the Government have proposed to set up two urban development corporations, modelled on the lines of the new town development corporations, to provide a single agency to mastermind the renewal of each area. The kind of machinery originally used to facilitate the planned dispersal of people from overcrowded conurbations is now being remodelled and adapted to facilitate the regeneration of two large inner urban areas and to attract people and industry back to them.

Betterment

Throughout the post-war period there has been one problem which has been the subject of much political controversy, and that is the problem of 'betterment'—i.e. the increase in land values attributable to development and the extent to which this should be reserved to the community. Labour Governments have made several attempts at legislation designed to ensure that development rights in land accrue to the community. The first attempt in the 1947 Act instituted a development charge of 100 per cent of the development value payable on the granting of planning permission. This was short-lived. A second attempt was made in 1967 when a Land Commission was established with powers to buy land compulsorily where it had already been established that it was ripe for development. The aim was to channel this land to those who would develop it. This too was short-lived. A more ambitious attempt was made by the then Government in the Community Land Act of 1975. Its objective was to place on local authorities the duty to acquire all land required for private development at current use value and to make it available to developers at market value. As a transitional arrangement authorities had the power to acquire land for development or redevelopment needed within 10 years. The Act is now being repealed. Conservative Governments have always felt that provisions of this nature could be seen as moves towards the nationalisation of land and have stressed the depressive effect on private development.

Ever since 1947, however, it has been accepted by all concerned that no compensation should be payable on refusal of planning permission for development. There is also a consensus now that the increase in land values created by the grant of a planning permission should be taxable. Interestingly enough the arrangements in the New Towns Act of 1946 which allow new town corporations to acquire land at values which exclude increases resulting from their own activities have remained unaltered and have worked well in the rather special circumstances of a clearly defined area designated as a new town.

Summary

To summarise, since the war British urban planning policies have traversed the whole gamut of urban renewal, using the term in its widest sense. Comprehensive redevelopment has given way to conservation and rehabilitation; dispersal policies have given way to policies designed to regenerate inner city areas and attract people and industry back to them.

Immediately after the war there was a remarkable consensus amongst all political parties and shades of public opinion that more housing was needed desperately; that people and jobs should be dispersed to new, self-contained urban environments to provide room for the reconstruction and remodelling of existing cities; but that those cities should be denied unrestricted expansion into the countryside through the establishment of green belts and strict control over the use and development of land.

During the 1950s major strides were made in fulfilling these objectives. New towns and planned expansions of existing towns catered for the planned dispersal of people and jobs from the large cities; green belts and strict development control coped in the main with the much larger voluntary exodus of people from those cities. There was a massive slum clearance programme, large-scale and comprehensive renewal of city centres, and much urban road building to cope with mounting traffic problems.

But the post-war consensus on town-planning objectives vanished in the turbulent 1960s. Plans for building very large new towns, and ambitious plans to modernise and reshape existing towns—all heavily influenced by the future population and traffic projections of that time—did not materialise, as public disquiet mounted over the quality of the new development and the social disruption which it created. There was increasing hostility over the whole process of large-scale comprehensive development of the existing urban fabric, and the disruptive effects of large-scale urban roads.

Reflecting marked changes in public attitudes, urban policies have swung from slum clearance to rehabilitation and gradual renewal in the housing field, from redevelopment to conservation in the wider urban scene, and from major new urban motorways to traffic management and small-scale, incremental improvements in the sphere of urban highways. Today they are heavily orientated towards conservation, rehabilitation and gradual renewal, with attention focussed on the complex environmental, social and economic problems of inner city areas.

Environmental determinism—the view that the creation of a pleasant physical environment would solve all problems—has given way to a clearer recognition of the complex interactions of town-planning, social and economic policies. Faith in regulative planning and state intervention is giving way to a clearer recognition of the necessity for, and value of, community participation and self-help in urban renewal processes.

It is tempting to predict that the 1980s will see a major onslaught on the problems of the inner areas in large cities and that policies of gradual urban renewal will develop, harnessing and guiding the ceaseless forces of change operating in every urban area. But a policy of gradual renewal is deceptively complex; it has its own sophistications, subtleties and pitfalls which have yet to unfold. Some of the lessons to be learnt from experience to date, some of the difficulties and pitfalls inherent in current policies and some of the emerging problems for the future are explored in the final chapter.

2

The urban environment

The British urban scene is one of sharp contrasts. There are many small towns and villages of unsurpassed and enduring charm. Then there are towns of unrelieved and depressing mediocrity. This dichotomy reflects not only the pace of the Industrial Revolution in the 19th century but also the fact that the urban settlements it created were in new locations and were not grafted on to the existing pre-industrial and basically agrarian pattern of settlements. These towns, hastily and haphazardly constructed, often in unsuitable locations, present complex urban environmental problems which differ from area to area.

Nowadays there is widespread concern about the need to improve and enhance the urban environment, and this is reflected in the growth of local amenity societies throughout the country.

For many years 'amenity' has been one of the most overworked words in town-planning language. Much has been done 'in the interests of amenity'; much has been forbidden as 'injurious to the interests of amenity'. Yet the word is nowhere defined in town-planning legislation. The dictionary definition is 'pleasantness' in manner, climate, or disposition. In town-planning usage it has been used to mean those elements in the appearance and layout of towns and countryside which are conducive to a pleasant and comfortable life rather than mere existence.

Since the 1960s 'amenity' has been increasingly subsumed by the elusive word 'environment'. Environment has been defined very widely as 'the moral, mental and material atmosphere that surrounds one from birth to death'. Modern usage of the word in the town-planning field does not go quite as wide as this, but it does include not only the appearance and layout of buildings but also all those parts of our physical surroundings which are liable to pollution in all its forms. Anything ugly, noisy, crowded, destructive and intrusive can affect the urban 'environment' and the quality of life in towns, and becomes a matter of concern. In this report the term 'environment' is used in this wider sense.

The importance attached to the urban environment can be seen in many ways—in the conservation of historic or architecturally important areas and buildings; in the quality of the design of new buildings; in efforts to alleviate urban dereliction and in policies to combat atmospheric pollution, noise and the impact of urban traffic. Action on all these fronts is necessary if the quality of urban life is to be improved and towns and cities made better places in which to live and work.

Conservation

The growth of the conservation movement has been described in chapter 1. It is now a dominant feature in policies designed to safeguard the urban environment. As already mentioned there are now over 4,000 conservation areas in towns and villages throughout the country.

This movement, which was further stimulated by the European Architectural Heritage campaign of 1975, reflects not only an awareness of the merit and quality of these older areas in towns but also disquiet over the destruction of the scale, variety and contrast in shopping centres in many towns and the disruption of whole communities following the massive slum clearance programme of the 1950s and early 1960s.

Within conservation areas there is a strong presumption against any new development unless it can be clearly shown to fit into the general character of the area. Conservation areas are providing a focus for concerted action aimed at improving the visual environment by removal of urban clutter in all its forms, by restoration and enhancement of the existing buildings and, where practicable, removal of traffic.

But conservation is not simply nostalgic preservation. It involves the far more complex processes of renovation, maintenance and enhancement of an area and finding new uses for the buildings concerned. It has been said that 'every Queen Anne front has a Mary Anne behind'. Behind elegant façades there may be small cafés, one-man businesses, scrap merchants, paint sprayers and a host of other activities occupying small, shabby, low-rented properties. The mews and the back streets are as important to the areas as the façades. If they are destroyed or wither away the whole area declines inexorably. Conservation is not an easy option if the character and the life of the area are to be preserved and adapted to changing economic circumstances.

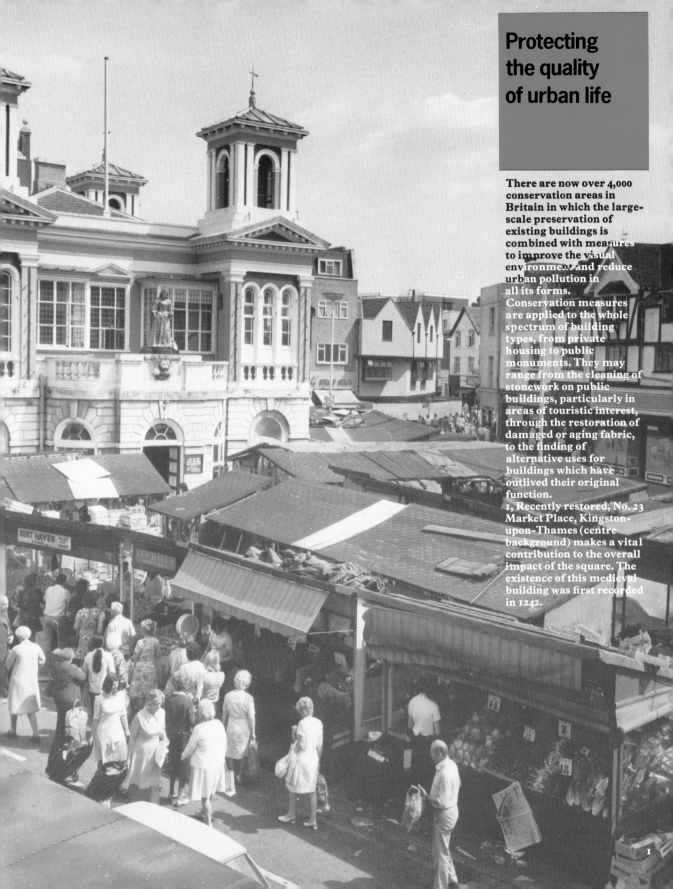

Protecting the quality of urban life

There are now over 4,000 conservation areas in Britain in which the large-scale preservation of existing buildings is combined with measures to improve the visual environment and reduce urban pollution in all its forms. Conservation measures are applied to the whole spectrum of building types, from private housing to public monuments. They may range from the cleaning of stonework on public buildings, particularly in areas of touristic interest, through the restoration of damaged or aging fabric, to the finding of alternative uses for buildings which have outlived their original function.

1, Recently restored, No. 23 Market Place, Kingston-upon-Thames (centre background) makes a vital contribution to the overall impact of the square. The existence of this medieval building was first recorded in 1242.

2,3, The Foreign and Commonwealth Office, London, before and after cleaning. 4, The Albert Memorial in Albert Square, Manchester, was badly eroded and structurally unsound before its recent restoration.

The restoration of medieval buildings can be particularly dramatic where the original timberwork is uncovered: 5,6, Bunyan's Mead, a late medieval street frontage at Elstow, Bedfordshire, before and after restoration.

7, St Paul's House, Park Square South, Leeds: a Victorian warehouse and factory with Moorish details, now renovated and turned into offices.

8, Piece Hall, Halifax, West Yorkshire: the former cloth market, built in the 1770s, was latterly used as the town's fruit and vegetable market. It has now been restored for use as a community centre, containing craft shops, an industrial museum, and a tourist information centre.

9

10

11

12

13

The small industrial town of Ironbridge, near Telford, Shropshire, has been turned into an industrial museum. Its centrepiece is the first iron bridge in the world, 9, built across the Severn in 1779. Other buildings have been preserved as museum pieces or converted to uses relevant to the museum

10, The Great Warehouse of the Coalbrookdale Company of Ironfounders, dating from the 1830s, was opened as the Iron Museum in 1979.

11, The Bedlam blast furnaces, in operation from the mid-18th to mid-19th centuries, were rescued from dereliction and opened to the public in 1979. 12, The Severn Warehouse, built in the 1840s as a riverside warehouse and subsequently used as a bicycle shop and garage, was restored to its 19th century condition and opened as an interpretation centre for the Ironbridge Gorge Museum in 1977.

13, The Hay Inclined Plane was formerly used to convey barges from the Shropshire Canal to the Coalport Canal and the River Severn below.

14

15

16

The residential areas of inner London owe much of their character to their Georgian and Victorian Terraces, many of which were until recently falling into dereliction. Large numbers of these terraces have now been restored and converted into flats by the local authorities.

14, Restoration of a terrace of houses on the Porchester Square Estate, Westminster.

15,16, The corner of Cloudesley Road and Batchelor Street, Islington, London—a typical Islington terrace before and after restoration.

17, Clifton Crescent, a restored and converted early Victorian terrace in Southwark, London.

17

The natural environment

It is now recognised that the careful preservation of buildings must be accompanied by the preservation of natural amenities such as water and trees: in recent years there has also been a concerted move to improve areas of urban wasteland.
1,2, At Anderston and Brommielaw Quay Gardens in Glasgow, a derelict site on the banks of the Clyde has been transformed into a leisure area.

3,4, Transformation of a typical back-street urban site at Eastleigh, Hampshire.
5,6, The creation of a children's playground near new housing on urban wasteland at St Aidan's Avenue, Blackburn.
Many developers now make an effort to preserve the existing landscape in new housing schemes.
7, A public housing scheme with shops at Runcorn New Town, Cheshire;
8, Private development at New Ash Green, Kent.

8

Design and external appearance of buildings

Although there has been a ready acceptance of the need to conserve buildings of merit, opinions are divided over the quality of post-war redevelopment. In particular, hostility has been directed at the tower blocks of flats and offices erected during this period.

Local planning authorities have powers to control the design and external appearance of buildings under the development control provisions of the Town and Country Planning legislation. In exercising these powers some authorities rely on their own qualified architects, others on panels drawn from members of the Royal Institute of British Architects and other bodies. In major cases, plans are referred to the Royal Fine Art Commission for their opinion.

Some local authorities have issued 'design guides' for developers and provoked controversy in doing so. The way in which this control has been exercised is a perennial subject for debate. There are those who argue that the impact of planning controls, whilst limiting abuses, has stifled creativity; that the pace of reconstruction was such that quality was sacrificed for quantity and that we have failed to produce redevelopment of real merit. On the other hand there are many examples of excellent schemes and new buildings which enhance the urban scene and which will doubtless be 'listed' for conservation by future generations. The debate continues.

If there is debate over the degree of aesthetic control of new urban development and on its quality, there is widespread acceptance of the value of cleaning, restoration and renovation of older buildings of architectural merit. Cleaning of buildings has become an important part in the restoration of our national heritage not only in London—Whitehall, Westminster Abbey, the Law Courts and the Tower—but also in other cities such as Manchester, Newcastle and Bradford, where washing away a century of industrial pollution has revealed the architectural details of many fine Victorian and Edwardian buildings.

There is also widespread interest in generally improving the appearance of drab urban areas, and 'face-lift' schemes have long been fostered by the Civic Trust. Today there are hundreds of such schemes resulting from co-operative action between local authorities and local amenity bodies.

Urban wasteland

Then there is the visual pollution created by unsightly and neglected vacant land within towns. Dereliction and decay is not simply concentrated in the inner city areas. It can pervade the environment of whole towns with insidious effect.

It has long been official policy to reclaim derelict land, and reclamation grants are available for its treatment. This is however land so damaged by industrial or other development that it is incapable of being used without treatment. It includes disused spoil heaps, worked-out mineral excavations, abandoned industrial installations and land affected by mining subsidence.

It is now recognised that, in addition to this derelict land, there is much dormant, under-used, or unused vacant land within most towns and cities which does not need expensive remedial treatment, but which is itself a form of urban pollution. Work done by the Civic Trust and local amenity societies under its auspices has shown that some of this land had remained neglected since the last century. A substantial amount however was created by premature demolition for housing and road schemes which were subsequently abandoned in the late 1960s and early 1970s. According to a report published by the Civic Trust in 1977, the land includes plots of all sizes, abandoned railway sidings, and vacant sites or buildings. Much of it is unsightly with rubbish, debris and rampant vegetation, and protected by ugly fencing. On the other hand some sites are an environmental asset rather than a liability—overgrown sites which mask derelict buildings, or a patch of wilderness that has become a breeding ground for butterflies. The report stated that there were opportunities to put this land (much of it publicly owned) to imaginative uses which could not fail to improve the urban environment.

The Government have launched a drive to make more use of this urban wasteland. A register of vacant and unused land owned by public authorities is to be set up and powers are being sought from Parliament to enable the Secretary of State to direct the sale of surplus land if public authorities refuse to make it available for sale when its retention is not clearly justified.

Industrial dereliction
the Lower Swansea Valley

Many of the problems facing British planners and conservationists are a direct legacy of the Industrial Revolution, and this is particularly evident in the Lower Swansea Valley in South Wales. Once the world centre of copper and zinc smelting, the Valley had by the 1950s become the largest single area of industrial dereliction in Britain. In the past two decades, extensive rehabilitation has been carried out. The Llansamlet Copper and Arsenic Works, left in ruins after its closure just before World War I, has been levelled and landscaped to form part of a Forest Park, 1,2. The semi-derelict Swansea Canal at Plasmarl, 3, photographed in 1968, has now been filled in and replaced by a by-pass, 4. 5, Children planting trees in a yearly exercise which involves over 100 pupils from 12 schools around the Valley.

Pollution in all its forms

The reduction of urban pollution in all its different forms can drastically improve the quality of urban life. The great London 'smog' of 1952, 1, aroused public awareness of the dangers of atmospheric pollution, and the Clean Air Act which followed in 1956 imposed stringent controls on smoke emission from domestic and industrial chimneys. 2,3, The effects of the Clean Air Act in Garstang, Liverpool. Urban traffic has long been a source of both noise and atmospheric pollution, 4, as is the more recent hazard of low-flying jet aircraft, 5.

ES TUESDAY DECE

CHAOS AGAIN IN FOG

LONDON QUEUE OF 3,000

MANY ROAD CRASHES

The fog which cleared from many areas of London during yesterday thickened again in the evening but an Air Ministry spokesman forecast last night that freshening winds would clear it everywhere to-day. It would then become cloudy with a little rain and milder.

West London areas cleared rapidly during the morning and there was brilliant sunshine. A light south-westerly breeze sprang up and the temperature rose from below freezing to 45deg. The breeze blew the fog eastwards to the Lea valley where it stayed. As a result most of east London, parts of Essex, and the Thames estuary experienced no improvement during the day.

By 6.30 p.m. London Transport reported an almost complete shut down of services in north-east London. Nearly all buses were at a standstill but the Underground was still running. A "complete blackout" extended from Wood Green to Highgate, Harringay, Enfield, Epping, Holloway, and Palmers Green. Conditions were almost as bad in parts of south-east London, including Blackwall Tunnel, Plumstead, Abbey Wood, Belvedere, Erith, and Bexley.

At the Central Line station at Stratford, after the bus services had stopped, 3,000 people were queuing for tickets at 5.30 p.m., and half an later the queue stretched for several yards.

2

3

SAY NO TO NOISE
DARLINGTON QUIET TOWN EXPERIMENT

9

5

4

Today, noise-reduction figures high on the list of planners' priorities, and is one reason for the extensive use of pedestrian schemes in both old and new town centres. 6,7, The High Street in Old Harlow, Essex, before and after pedestrianisation.
The public body responsible for matters of noise in Britain is the Noise Advisory Council. In 1976 it initiated a two-year 'quiet town experiment' at Darlington, Co. Durham, which involved an intensive campaign against noise at home, at work and in public, and relied on the active participation of many different parts of the community, 8,9.

The Industrial Revolution has left a legacy of dereliction in many older towns. One such area is the lower Swansea valley in South Wales where the defoliation created by copper smelting and the pollution created by the metallurgical industry in the last century have resulted in one of the most concentrated areas of dereliction in the United Kingdom. This is now being transformed through the joint action of central and local government and through community action. There are plans to create, in this key area close to the town, modern industrial estates interspersed with urban parks and regional sports facilities. Waste tips have been cleared, vegetation re-established and obsolete buildings put to new uses. Newly planted trees were at first vandalised but a policy of involving local community groups, instead of simply fencing and patrolling the areas, has proved successful and has awakened local interest and enthusiasm. The local authority now see the area as one of economic opportunity, with new industrial development making a vital contribution to the economic well-being of the city as well as achieving a quite dramatic improvement of the environment.

Trees

Planting and preserving trees in urban areas has long been official policy. Powers to make tree preservation orders were given to local planning authorities in the 1947 Town and Country Planning Act, and comprehensive guidance was given to those authorities as long ago as 1958 in a book called *Trees in town and country,* published by the Ministry of Housing and Local Government. This gave detailed suggestions on the use of trees in urban areas, in connection with both redevelopment and new development, together with extensive advice on the choice and care of trees suitable for towns.

Trees are an important element in the urban scene. They add variety, movement and colour to streets and squares, hiding eyesores and softening the hard and sometimes ugly outlines of man-made structures. Today it is standard practice when giving planning permission for new development for local planning authorities to insist on effective landscaping arrangements and the preservation of any significant trees on the site. When judiciously used along major lines of communication, such as urban motorways and railway lines, trees can enhance our important initial impressions of environmental quality on entering a locality. A love of, and respect for, trees seems ingrained in the national character, going back to the great landscape-gardening traditions of the 18th century. Many millions of new trees were planted throughout the land during a national 'Plant a Tree' campaign in 1973.

Clean air

The unpleasant conditions in Victorian industrial towns led to an early interest in control over atmospheric pollution. The first Alkali Act was passed as early as 1863 to control industrial processes which gave off hydrochloric acid. These controls were progressively extended to cover activities in the chemical, metal manufacturing, ceramic and allied industries. The Alkali Inspectorate, established as a government agency to control registered industrial processes, was probably one of the world's first pollution control agencies.

Even so there was no effective control over smoke from domestic and industrial chimneys until 1956. In a coal-burning economy, smoke pollution grew. It took a cataclysmic 'smog' in London in 1952, which has been estimated to have been responsible for over 4,000 deaths from bronchial and respiratory diseases, to arouse public opinion fully to the growing health hazards of atmospheric pollution. An expert Committee was set up and a Clean Air Act followed in 1956. The Act was a milestone in control over atmospheric pollution. Responsibility for clean air was given to local authorities (the renamed Alkali and Clean Air Inspectorate retained control over particularly offensive and dangerous industrial emissions). The local authorities were able to declare 'smoke control areas' within which the emission of smoke from chimneys became an offence, and subsidies were given to help convert appliances to cope with smokeless fuels. The emission of dark smoke from any trade or industrial premises or from the chimney of any building was in general prohibited. The height of chimneys serving new furnaces is controlled and approved grit and dust arrestment plant has to be installed.

These stringent controls have led to a dramatic improvement in the quality of air in towns and cities. Over half the premises in the conurbations are now covered by smoke control areas. Average urban concentrations of smoke have been reduced by about 80 per cent since 1960. Dense, smoke-laden 'smogs' are now a thing of the past. Winter sunshine levels in central London and cities such as Glasgow and Sheffield have increased by 70 per cent since 1958. Concentrations of sulphur dioxide have been reduced by 40 per cent in the last 10 years, again mainly due to domestic smoke control. Roses in suburban gardens are now developing 'black spot', which was hitherto held in check by this pollution. Clean air is one very noticeable improvement in the urban environment.

In more recent years attention has been focussed on traffic fumes. Controls now exist over emissions from motor vehicles. The maximum permitted lead content of petrol has been reduced from 0.84 grammes per litre to 0.45 grammes. There is to be a further reduction to 0.4 grammes from 1 January 1981.

Noise

Nowadays noise is widely recognised as a form of pollution. As such it is being subjected to a two-pronged attack—measures designed to reduce noise at its source and measures designed to protect people from its effects.

People had long been aware of industrial noise, for dirty and noisy industry had sat cheek by jowl with housing in the 19th century towns. This had a powerful influence on the planning of the first wave of new towns, where industrial estates were carefully segregated from residential areas.

Public consciousness of noise as a pollutant did not however come to a head until the beginning of the 1960s. There was mounting annoyance at the growing volume of traffic noise in urban areas and at aircraft noise, which increased markedly with the growth in the use of jet engines in passenger aircraft. There was also considerable annoyance over the noise created by demolition and new building—yet another consequence of the scale and pace of urban reconstruction.

Nowadays efforts are being made to reduce noise at its source, for example through legislation on the noise levels produced by aircraft and motor vehicles. Measures are also being instituted to protect people from the effects of noise, and these include the careful siting of new residential development away from sources of noise, the soundproofing of housing subject to excessive aircraft or traffic noise, and regulations on noise insulation in the internal design of attached houses and flats.

Local authorities are responsible for the enforcement of noise control and are required to inspect their areas for noise nuisance and to take action to reduce it. They have been given powers in a wide-ranging Control of Pollution Act passed in 1974 to set up 'noise abatement zones' within which they can exercise additional controls over noise from premises in specified categories. There are also provisions to control noise from construction and demolition sites.

A 'quiet town experiment' has been sponsored at Darlington, which was probably the first of its kind in the world. It involved an intensive campaign, spread over two years, to reduce noise levels at home, at work and in public places by means of education, publicity and experimental schemes. The scheme relied on local initiatives and the active involvement of all concerned—schools, transport undertakings, trade councils, etc. The scheme was not an experiment in the strict scientific sense since no attempt was made to measure objectively whether noise levels were actually reduced as a result of the campaign. The scheme did show, however, that a local council, given sufficient imagination and enthusiasm—but at very little expense— could gain the interest of a large proportion of its citizens in the problem of noise. In particular the scheme demonstrated considerable scope for involving school children in concern about noise. The Noise Advisory Council, which initiated and directed the 'quiet town experiment', is publishing a full report on it during 1980.

In the field of air pollution it is possible to give some statistical measures of achievements to date. It is not yet possible to do this on urban noise levels. Government forecasts indicate good prospects for a reduction in the number of houses exposed to very high levels of aircraft noise, as noisy older planes are phased out. There is no firm evidence that noise from fixed sources—industry, construction and neighbouring households— is changing much in objective terms, but complaints show an upward trend, which may reflect a degree of public sensitivity to intrusive noise. In the case of road traffic, the benefits of reducing noise from individual vehicles are likely to be offset by increasing traffic flows. Traffic could continue to be the dominant noise problem for many years.

Urban traffic

Many people would regard traffic as the greatest source of urban pollution. Traffic noise, particularly the noise of heavy lorries; traffic fumes; the visual impact of vehicles

Durham –
conserving an historic city

The harmonious combination of conservation measures with careful redevelopment is now seen as the key to preserving the character of Britain's historic towns. This approach is typified by the programme which has been carried forward over the past six years in the City of Durham. Extensive pedestrianisation schemes in the city centre have improved its accessibility to many thousands of visitors, and planning restrictions on new development have ensured that this conforms with existing architectural styles and materials.

There has been particular emphasis on preserving open views both of and from the central area. The diagram illustrates the complex planning required for such a comprehensive scheme. 1,2, Silver Street, Durham, before and after pedestrianisation. 3,4, Reconstruction of a

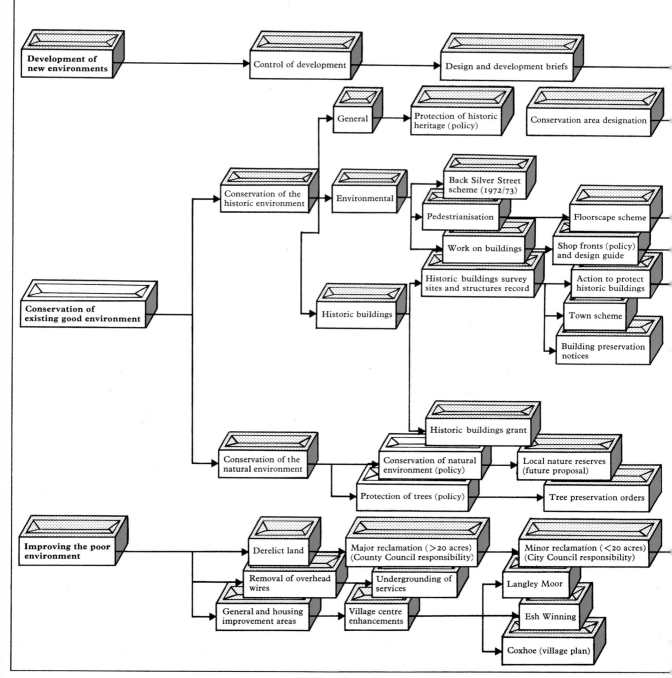

- **Development of new environments** → Control of development → Design and development briefs

- **Conservation of existing good environment**
  - Conservation of the historic environment
    - General → Protection of historic heritage (policy) · Conservation area designation
    - Environmental
      - Back Silver Street scheme (1972/73)
      - Pedestrianisation → Floorscape scheme
      - Work on buildings → Shop fronts (policy) and design guide
    - Historic buildings → Historic buildings survey sites and structures record
      - Action to protect historic buildings
      - Town scheme
      - Building preservation notices
  - Conservation of the natural environment
    - Historic buildings grant
    - Conservation of natural environment (policy) → Local nature reserves (future proposal)
    - Protection of trees (policy) → Tree preservation orders

- **Improving the poor environment**
  - Derelict land → Major reclamation (>20 acres) (County Council responsibility) → Minor reclamation (<20 acres) (City Council responsibility)
  - Removal of overhead wires → Undergrounding of services → Langley Moor
  - General and housing improvement areas → Village centre enhancements → Esh Winning
  - Coxhoe (village plan)

14th century building in the Milburngate Shopping Centre. 5, A view of Durham's historic centre, dominated by the Castle and the Cathedral.

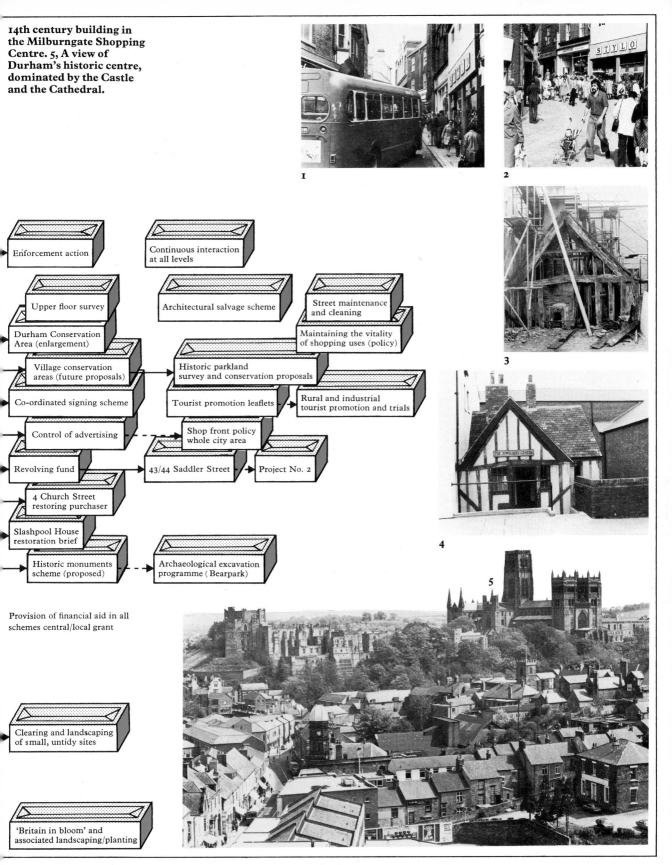

Enforcement action

Continuous interaction at all levels

Upper floor survey

Architectural salvage scheme

Street maintenance and cleaning

Durham Conservation Area (enlargement)

Maintaining the vitality of shopping uses (policy)

Village conservation areas (future proposals)

Historic parkland survey and conservation proposals

Co-ordinated signing scheme

Tourist promotion leaflets

Rural and industrial tourist promotion and trials

Control of advertising

Shop front policy whole city area

Revolving fund

43/44 Saddler Street

Project No. 2

4 Church Street restoring purchaser

Slashpool House restoration brief

Historic monuments scheme (proposed)

Archaeological excavation programme (Bearpark)

Provision of financial aid in all schemes central/local grant

Clearing and landscaping of small, untidy sites

'Britain in bloom' and associated landscaping/planting

1

2

3

4

5

parked in almost every nook and cranny or herded into large, ugly, utilitarian multi-storey garages which contribute nothing architecturally to the townscape—all these things offend our senses and detract from the quality of urban life.

Yet the efficient and convenient movement of goods and services throughout a town is vital to its economic well-being. Without it, prosperity can ebb away. The car is an essential and cherished possession; it permits personal and flexible movement for all sorts of purposes. It has become an indispensable element in modern life, despite the fact that many people do not have access to a car—in particular the aged or the very young—and must therefore rely heavily on public transport.

This basic dilemma was analysed in Sir Colin Buchanan's report *Traffic in towns*, which was published in 1963. The concepts advocated in that report—the creation of primary road networks where traffic is given precedence and environmental areas where traffic is subordinated to the needs of those living and working there—have not been fully tried out. The swing of public opinion against urban road building aborted attempts to provide fully fledged primary road networks. Nevertheless much has been done in creating traffic-free pedestrian precincts in the shopping centres of many towns, and in routeing heavy traffic away from residential areas. The emphasis on traffic management and the need to make the maximum use of existing road frameworks has stimulated great ingenuity in the devising of schemes to keep open the movement arteries in urban areas. Inevitably this has been at the cost of urban clutter, most notably an ever-increasing volume of road signs and instructions to motorists, pedestrians and those using public transport. Traffic 'graffiti' abound throughout towns and cities.

The problem of reconciling efficient movement of traffic in all its forms with good living conditions remains unresolved. There are no easy, universally applicable solutions, otherwise they would have been found long ago. Yet the effects of urban traffic remain one of the biggest impediments to any campaign of urban renaissance.

Change and diversity

Urban environments differ, but they are all subject to change, and in this process all the factors so far described in this chapter are important. Clean air and less noise; strenuous and imaginative use of urban wasteland combined with control over the quality of new development; conservation which enhances rather than ossifies; and measures which reduce the effect of urban traffic without restricting the efficient movement of people, goods and services—all these are important improvements to urban living.

The quality of urban life is an elusive concept. It is more than the sum of all these parts, important though they may be. It embraces the 'polity' of the town—the vigour and vision of its municipal leadership and its responsiveness to the needs of the deprived and more vulnerable citizens. It embraces the town's economy; its employment and social structure; the quality of its education and other community services; and above all the aspirations and interests of the people living there. In short the quality of urban life can be as diverse and rich as life itself.

Durham is but one example of a town determinedly pursuing policies to upgrade the urban environment. Here the local authority has come to regard its custodial role for the city as 'looking to the future but caring for the past', and actively practises what might be termed 'good husbandry'. Based on an integrated three-fold approach—seeking quality in new development, conserving good quality existing areas and improving poor ones—action is already well advanced in the historic central area. It is hoped that a feeling of 'pride of place', generated by the care and attention being shown in the city's architecturally and historically important centre, will stimulate interest in environmental improvement elsewhere in the city.

Urban renewal is ceaseless. It presents an unremitting challenge to local leadership and to the people living in towns. The problem of how to harness and guide effectively the constant processes of change is by no means resolved. The prospect is one of accelerating change and deepening uncertainty about future trends. All this puts a premium on urban plans and policies that are flexible and readily adaptable to ever changing circumstances. It also puts a premium on measures which encourage civic pride and awareness and public participation by creative local activity—a theme which will be dealt with in chapter 5.

3

Housing renewal

The housing shortage

The provision of good, well-designed housing in a good environment, reasonably near to places of work or in areas where people want to live, and available at acceptable cost, is a basic urban planning objective, however difficult it may be to achieve.

Throughout most of this century, until the 1970s, the housing scene in the United Kingdom has been dominated by a shortage of houses in relation to the number of households. Since 1901 the population has grown by 40 per cent. During the same period the number of households has more than doubled. Families have become smaller; there are more one-person households and far less sharing of houses by three generations. Add to this the legacy of the Industrial Revolution, the hiatus in house-building during two world wars and the damage caused by World War II, and it is clear that the pressing need was to build as many houses as quickly as possible throughout the country.

National housing conditions have been transformed in the post-war period. In 1951 there were 750,000 more households than houses in England and Wales. By 1976 there were 500,000 more houses than households. About 7 million new dwellings have been built since the war. More than two families in every five now live in a post-war home. On the basis of indicators such as basic amenities and amount of overcrowding, Britain has better housing than most other countries.

There has also been a major social change in housing tenure. At the end of World War I about 90 per cent of the housing stock was privately rented and the rest owner-occupied. Even in 1951, 52 per cent was still privately rented, 31 per cent was owner-occupied and the public sector (local-authority, new-town and housing-association housing) accounted for 17 per cent. By 1976 owner-occupation dominated with 55 per cent of the total; the public sector amounted to 30 per cent and the privately rented sector had contracted to 15 per cent. This major shift to house ownership has been paralleled with much greater security of tenure for those living in rented accommodation.

Current housing problems

Clearly, much has been achieved in the field of housing. But this does not mean that there are no longer any problems. A government housing review published in 1977 stated: 'In 1951, there were nearly 10 million households in England and Wales—families with children, childless couples and people on their own—living in physically unsatisfactory conditions or sharing accommodation. By 1976 the figure had probably fallen to about 2.7 million and there was no longer an absolute shortage of houses. These figures are a cause for both satisfaction and concern: satisfaction that so much has been done; concern that much remains to be done. The continuing improvement in national housing conditions is no consolation to people who remain in poor conditions. On the contrary their problems are thrown into sharp relief.'

The problems now thrown into sharp relief are the decaying environment in the inner areas of the large cities and the housing problems of groups of people who may experience special difficulties in getting suitable housing—the lower income households, homeless people, one-parent families, disabled and handicapped people, old people, single people, mobile workers and ethnic minorities. The housing problem continues, but in a different and more complex form, intertwined with issues of social and economic deprivation and the problems of some of the most vulnerable members of society.

Finally, housing renewal (again using the term in its widest sense) has no finite solution. It is as ceaseless and continuous as urban renewal itself. The same government review quoted above foresaw the longer-term picture as follows:
'The picture emerging . . . is one of a continued reduction in the amount of unfit and substandard housing but an increasing incidence of major disrepair. We are no longer faced with massive areas of unfit housing, though some substantial clearance programmes remain. But if we are to prevent the emergence of a new generation of slum areas, housing policy will have to place growing emphasis on the repair, maintenance and effective use of the existing stock.'
It is against this general background that current policies of house improvement, area rehabilitation and gradual renewal need to be considered.

Post-war planners sought to solve the problem of urban dereliction by demolishing large tracts of decayed housing and replacing them with massive new estates. But this new urban environment often proved far from ideal for the inhabitants. The hazards of decaying fabric, overcrowding and inadequate toilet facilities were replaced by those of social alienation, vandalism and lack of play facilities for children in high-rise blocks. Today, the shortcomings of much post-war redevelopment have been recognised, and this recognition has brought a radical change in housing policies and design.

1,2, Slum housing ripe for demolition at Popham Street, Islington, London, and Boundary Street, Liverpool.

3, The problems of living in a high-rise block: boys playing football in a stair-well on the Pepys Estate, Lewisham, London.

4, Urban dereliction alongside comprehensive redevelopment in Liverpool.

Housing for the 1980s

The British have traditionally shown a preference for living in houses rather than flats, and for many of them a private garden rates as a necessity. Present-day housing in Britain reflects an awareness of these traditional needs, aiming to provide a comfortable environment and foster a sense of community. Even where considerations of scale and density limit. individual space, architects have sought to humanise their schemes by the use of traditional building materials and of architectural details designed to break the monotony of facades.

Some modern interpretations of the traditional urban terrace: 1, A development owned by the City of Birmingham at Bristol Road, Edgbaston; 2, a housing association development of flats at Lonsdale Place, Islington, London; these two developments received a Civic Trust Award and Commendation respectively in 1979. 3, Public-sector housing including units for the disabled at Ludwick Mews, Lewisham, London. The new towns provide obvious scope for adventurous housing design. 4,5, Public-sector rented housing at Neath Hill and Linford, both in the new town of Milton Keynes.

8

10

A number of bodies in Britain make awards for good design in housing and other architectural fields, among them the Royal Institute of British Architects and the Civic Trust. The Awards for Good Design in Housing made annually by the Department of the Environment aim to encourage varying solutions to a wide range of housing needs: 6, Flats owned by the London Borough of Merton at Watermeads, Rawnsley Avenue, Mitcham (medal winner, 1979).
7,8, A public scheme at Field Court, Fitzjohn's Avenue, London NW3, (highly commended, 1980).
9, A development of private houses at Lakeside Drive, Esher, Surrey (medal winner, 1980).
10, Old people's housing at Sudbury Court, Peterborough, Cambridgeshire (medal winner, 1979). The developments at Bristol Road, Edgbaston, 1, and Queensway, Cambridge 11, were both highly commended in 1979, while the development for disabled people at Ludwick Mews, Lewisham, 3, was highly commended in 1980.

11

One of the most original recent solutions to the problem of large scale public housing is the Byker development in Newcastle. The main feature of the 81 ha (200 acre) site is the undulating Wall, which presents a blank face to a motorway on its north side, while the southern face, 14, is given human scale and variety by the addition of wooden balconies, 13, painted in bright colours. The adjoining low-rise housing, 12, provides an intimate and colourful environment. A similar use of wooden balconies is found in a public development of flats at Queensway, Trumpington Road, Cambridge, 11.

12

13

14

House improvement

Until the 1960s house improvement did not figure as an important element in housing policies. The national imperatives were to deal with the national housing shortage and clear away the slums. Older housing, whether fit or unfit, was regarded as having a strictly limited life. The life cycle for housing areas was seen as one of development, decay, clearance and then redevelopment. Improvement of houses in areas that were clearly going downhill was considered to be throwing away good money after bad. 'Patching' of houses was a strictly temporary makeshift policy to alleviate intolerable living conditions until new housing became available in the redevelopment areas. Improvement grants when made were largely confined to better housing with a demonstrably long life. There was no policy for tackling house improvement on an area basis combined with simultaneous improvement of the environment of the residential areas.

House improvement in its widest sense was of course being carried out through private initiatives. As households became better off they either moved to other homes with more space or chose to extend their existing homes. There was a steady flow of applications for planning permission for domestic garages and extensions to houses. By the beginning of the 1960s these were running at a rate of over 50,000 applications a year for garages and over 80,000 a year for 'other' classes of development (excluding new development).

The shift in the climate of opinion and in urban planning policies which took place in the 1960s and early 1970s has already been described in its wider urban context in chapter 1. This was the period which saw the relinquishment of large-scale comprehensive redevelopment in favour of conservation and rehabilitation. On the housing front this meant a move away from massive slum clearance to housing improvement on an area basis and gradual renewal.

Several factors contributed to this change of policy. A detailed national House Condition Survey in 1967 revealed the depths and complications of housing renewal and shattered the concept that all slums could be cleared away to a set time-scale. Academic studies were querying the rather simplistic concepts about the 'life' of houses and residential areas. There was no longer a national housing shortage; the total housing stock now exceeded the number of households. Rising costs and inflation made improvement economically more desirable than redevelopment. The Buchanan Report, *Traffic in towns*, had introduced the concept of environmental areas. Some local authorities such as Leeds had been experimenting with concentrating house-improvement grants on an area basis and coupling this with measures to upgrade the environment. The Ministry of Housing and Local Government (as it then was) was conducting its studies into suitable renewal policies for the so-called 'twilight' areas and had published in 1966 its study on Deeplish. This was a small residential area in Rochdale in Lancashire, close to the town centre, where a strong community spirit prevailed. The study led to the implementation of a scheme in co-operation with the local authority, which demonstrated what could be done at modest cost not only to improve individual houses but also to raise the whole tone of the area by clearing away rubbish, re-routeing traffic, providing play spaces, etc. Above all there was a massive popular revulsion against the disruptive effects of large-scale slum clearance, which had destroyed whole communities and the economy of the areas concerned. Public disfavour was particularly focussed on the new tower blocks by the Ronan Point disaster of 1968, in which a gas explosion caused the partial collapse of a 22-storey block of flats in east London.

General improvement areas

In 1968 the Government of the day published a White Paper entitled *Old houses into new homes,* and in 1969 a Housing Act widened the scope of house improvement grants, increased their value and gave local authorities a discretionary power to declare 'general improvement areas' (GIAs). Within GIAs there were grants covering 50 per cent of eligible expenses (subsequently raised to 60 per cent) and central government and local authority grants for environmental improvement up to a limit of £100 (and later £200) per dwelling. The local authorities were given somewhat wider powers to assist and persuade owners to improve houses and to buy land and houses needed for area improvement.

GIAs are intended to be areas of fundamentally sound houses capable of providing good living conditions for many years to come and unlikely to be affected by redevelopment or other major planning proposals. They should be areas free of housing stress, with stable communities, offering scope for creating a better environment. By December 1979 there were a total of 1,208 GIAs in operation containing nearly 400,000 houses, spread throughout the country, and there is some evidence to suggest that the decline of these areas has been halted.

A housing area in Macclesfield provides an interesting example of what can be done. In 1971 an architect bought a house in Black Road, Macclesfield. This was an area comprising some 300 statutorily unfit houses built around 1815 and designated for slum clearance. Under his aegis, a local action group was formed which led in 1973 to an area of 32 houses being declared a GIA. The local authority provided funds for environmental works; gave maximum improvement grants where possible; carried out necessary legal work; supplied mortgages; relaxed standards and public health by-law controls; and made available temporary accommodation for residents whilst improvements to their houses were being done. The residents contributed the remainder of the money needed and as a self-help group (with the assistance also of friends and relatives) acted as general contractors. The work was completed in the autumn of 1974 with every house improved to the standard required for grants, giving a minimum life of 30 years both to the dwellings and the environment. The Black Road GIA is in an area which has since been declared a conservation area, and later work on the scheme has won its architect one of the 1980 awards in the Belgian Institute of Housing's Prix International d'Architecture.

The rate of take-up of grants increased following the 1969 Housing Act. In 1971 it rose sharply following the temporary provision of a 75 per cent rate of grant in those parts of the country in which various measures had been taken to mitigate the effects of economic decline. In 1973 the rate of grants in the UK peaked at 450,000. Since then it has steadily declined in the main as a consequence of the success of the policy. Dwellings which still lack basic amenities are those in the worst general condition and occupied by households least able, especially in the prevailing economic climate, to finance their share of the cost of improvement.

As so often happens, however, solutions to one set of problems exposed new and different problems. Over 80 per cent of the grants went to owner-occupied and local authority housing, and most of these were outside the GIAs. Landlords proved reluctant to make use of improvement grants unless they could first obtain vacant possession of the property. This was a period when house prices were rising fast. Some landlords were evicting tenants, improving their property with the aid of grants and then selling it to owner-occupiers. There was a feeling that the system was being misused and was intensifying housing stress by adding to a shortage of housing to rent.

Housing action areas

In response to the problems outlined above, a Housing Act in 1974 introduced the concept of 'housing action areas' (HAAs). These are areas where poor housing is combined with social stress and deprivation. The aim is to secure an improvement in living conditions in existing houses as quickly as possible within a five-year period while keeping the local community together. There are now at least 411 HAAs in operation containing over 115,000 dwellings.

Currently there are four types of renovation grant:
a) grants for carrying out house improvements to a high standard or for conversion into flats;
b) intermediate grants for the provision of standard amenities and associated repairs;
c) special grants (not available in Scotland) for providing standard amenities in houses of multiple occupation; and
d) repairs grants available only in HAAs and GIAs.
The scale of these grants depends on the location of the dwelling—up to 75 per cent (90 per cent in cases of hardship) of eligible expenses in HAAs; up to 60 per cent in GIAs and up to 50 per cent elsewhere.
A government contribution amounting to 75 per cent (90 per cent in HAAs and GIAs) of each grant is paid to the local authority. In GIAs there is a specific grant of £200 per dwelling for environmental improvement; in HAAs it is £50, the concept being that HAAs can in due course be upgraded to GIA status. There are broadly similar arrangements in Scotland, but there the term general improvement area is not used and HAA powers are available for areas in which at least half the houses fail to meet prescribed physical standards.

House improvement and gradual renewal

In the last two decades, it has been recognised that preserving the fabric of inner city areas is a way of preserving the community life which was often disrupted by massive redevelopment. The improvement of existing housing, rather than demolition and redevelopment, is now seen as both socially and economically desirable, and 'general improvement areas' and 'housing action areas' have been created in which substantial house improvement grants are available.

One of the earliest GIA's, Deeplish in Rochdale, Lancashire, was the subject of an exhaustive government study in 1966, which covered details such as landscaping and street furniture as well as the fabric of the houses themselves. 1,2, An artist's impressions, from the Deeplish Study, of improvements to the front of a typical terrace, and to a back alley. 3, Pomona Street after improvement in 1969.

1

2

3

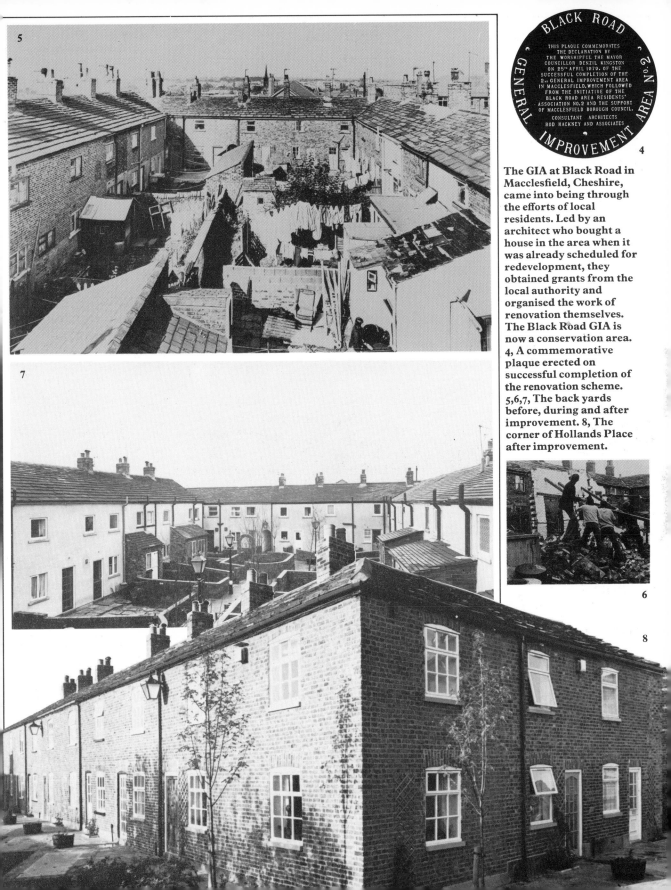

5

7

4

The GIA at Black Road in
Macclesfield, Cheshire,
came into being through
the efforts of local
residents. Led by an
architect who bought a
house in the area when it
was already scheduled for
redevelopment, they
obtained grants from the
local authority and
organised the work of
renovation themselves.
The Black Road GIA is
now a conservation area.
4, A commemorative
plaque erected on
successful completion of
the renovation scheme.
5,6,7, The back yards
before, during and after
improvement. 8, The
corner of Hollands Place
after improvement.

6

8

Even where redevelopment is unavoidable, this is done gradually and on a small scale, so that it does not radically alter the character of a neighbourhood. The Jericho area in Oxford, declared a GIA in 1975, is an example of 'gradual renewal' in action.
9,10, Nos 9-20 Nelson Street, before and after redevelopment, which included removal of the local parish hall.
11,12, 'Infill' development in Albert Street. 13,14, Redevelopment in Great Clarendon Street in which an old school house was preserved. 15,16, New housing on a former factory site in Canal Street.

9   10

11   12

13   14

Gradual renewal makes extensive use of 'infill' building – small scale developments which plug a gap in existing building and are carefully designed not to strike a discordant note.
17,18, Two examples of infill development which are uncompromisingly modern, yet blend well with their historic surroundings: undergraduate rooms at Brasenose College, Oxford, and flats at Hanover Court in the conservation area of Plymouth Barbican. A development in Middle Church Lane, Farnham, 19,20, uses the local colour of brick to merge discreetly into its surroundings.

15   16

60

17

19   20

18

A development of flats
replacing three houses in
Eddystone Terrace,
Plymouth, 21, provides a
modern interpretation of
the terrace's style. A
large-scale renewal
scheme in the village of
Newhaven, 22, near
Edinburgh, combines
conservation with new
housing which employs
traditional architectural
features.

The preservation and
conversion of existing
buildings are an essential
part of gradual renewal,
and London's dockland
area has benefited from
the conversion of many of
its old warehouses into
studios, craft workshops
and flats. The Ivory House
at St Katherine's Dock,
near the Tower of London,
23, has been completely
restored to provide
luxury service apartments,
shops and offices as well as
a yacht club and library.
It is part of a
comprehensive scheme
which includes a new hotel
and new housing, shops
and a pub.

Currently, changes designed to remove unnecessary restrictions are being made to the system of renovation grants in housing legislation going through Parliament. For example, proposals to install basic amenities such as a bath or inside toilets can attract a grant without requiring the occupant to carry out comprehensive improvement. Also, local authorities are being given more flexibility in administering the scheme and to adjust the levels of grant according to the income of the householder.

The 1974 Act also introduced the concept of compulsory improvement within HAAs. Local authorities were given powers to serve provisional improvement notices on landlords who are unwilling voluntarily to improve their properties. They also have powers to acquire compulsorily property in disrepair, where those responsible are unwilling or unable to rehabilitate it; where housing in multiple occupation is unsatisfactorily managed or prejudices the improvement of groups of dwellings; or where housing is being kept unreasonably empty. The emphasis remains however on voluntary rather than compulsory improvement.

There have been some criticisms of the GIA and HAA concepts—namely that the area approach does not help those in need of housing outside those areas; that there is still too much emphasis on house improvement and too little on environmental improvement; and that the poorer households within these areas are unable to afford their share of improvement costs or are unwilling to accept the disturbance involved, particularly if they are elderly.

There are of course problems, but the whole approach does represent a significant break with the past. The HAA concept does import a social dimension into housing improvement, seen most clearly in the policies which have evolved in the inner areas of cities where many of the HAAs are in any case located. Constraints on public expenditure naturally inhibit the extent to which local authorities can take action to improve the environment of the areas concerned. When they do, this can promote confidence in the longer-term future of the area, and house owners and landlords are encouraged to undertake expenditure on improvements because the costs will be recouped in due course by a rise in property values. Present problems and difficulties do not however invalidate what has become known as the policy of 'gradual renewal'.

Gradual renewal

As already mentioned in chapter 1, 'gradual renewal' has been defined as a continuous process of minor rebuilding and renovation, sustaining and reinforcing the vitality of a neighbourhood in ways which are responsive to changing social and physical needs. It involves a sensitive and fine-tuned approach to the housing problems and needs of the residential areas concerned, unobtrusive, small-scale new building, and a willingness to apply varying standards of improvement to houses to meet the wishes of the inhabitants rather than attempting to apply uniform standards throughout the chosen area. It can be slow and time-consuming, but in the long run it is likely to have more lasting effects because it is more closely linked to the varied needs of the inhabitants.

The Jericho district in the city of Oxford is but one example of the way in which the process works. This is a largely self-contained area close to the city centre, consisting for the most part of 19th century terraced housing built to a variety of standards and house types by many different builders. The area had been slipping downhill, with over half the housing clearly unfit and a further 40 per cent bordering on unfitness. It appeared to be an obvious subject for comprehensive clearance and redevelopment, but strong opposition had developed to this proposal. A social survey carried out by the local authority in 1976 revealed a stable community wishing to stay in the area, and in their own houses, because of its nearness to the town centre, the cheapness of the housing and the proximity of friends and relations. Wholesale clearance was clearly unacceptable. But the housing was of such poor quality that comprehensive improvement was uneconomic and could not be justified. Detailed social surveys established which people were willing to move, provided that this would be into another old terraced house, who would be happy to accept a new dwelling but in the same area, and the few who would be prepared to be rehoused elsewhere. An assessment was also made of the demands and resources for improvement amongst individual owners and tenants. Some were willing to undertake full-scale improvement; others were adamant that they would neither improve nor move.

As and when opportunities arose the local authority proceeded to buy houses by agreement and not by compulsion. Some were renovated to full standard to set an example, while the worst old houses were pulled down and replaced by small pockets of new housing carefully designed to fit into the grain of the area. Those who were prepared to improve their property were encouraged to do so; those who did not were left alone. Small environmental improvements were made along the streets, and there are plans to replace, again on a small scale, some of the outworn facilities.

The result has been a steady upgrading of the area as confidence about its future has grown. The blighting effects of comprehensive redevelopment have been avoided; so has unwarranted expenditure on comprehensive improvements to uniform standards. The stability of the community has been preserved and the choice of housing in age, price, and tenure increased. While compulsion has been avoided, attitudes to renewal have changed. The process has been slow and painstaking, but effective. This experience of gradual renewal may well have important lessons and applications in the wider urban scene.

Massive slum clearance has given way to housing and environmental improvement, in the form of general improvement areas and housing action areas, involving far less social disruption. These policies have not been free from problems and difficulties. The gradual renewal approach—entailing small-scale, sensitive redevelopment coupled with selective house renovation and environmental improvements, all closely attuned to the wishes and needs of the local inhabitants— may be slow and undramatic, but could well prove in the longer term to be the most effective form of urban renewal. It links with the growing awareness of the need to improve the quality of urban life described in chapter 2 and with the trends towards creative public participation described in chapter 5.

Summary

To summarise, there has been a striking improvement in the national housing stock since the end of the war. More than two families out of every five now live in a post-war house. Housing standards have greatly improved and, in terms of basic amenities and incidence of overcrowding, Britain has better housing than most other countries. There has been a major shift in house-tenure. Privately rented housing now constitutes only 15 per cent of the total stock, compared with 52 per cent at the end of the war. There has been a polarisation into owner-occupation (55 per cent) and public sector, mainly rented, accommodation (30 per cent).

There may no longer be a national shortage of houses, but the housing problems that remain are difficult and complex. There is the question of housing for groups experiencing special difficulties—the lower income groups, one-parent families, disabled and handicapped people, the elderly, the young single people, mobile workers and the ethnic minorities. Housing policy has become involved in problems of social and economic deprivation and not simply with the question of the physical state of the nation's housing stock. There are the decaying inner areas to be considered and beyond this the looming problems of disrepair.

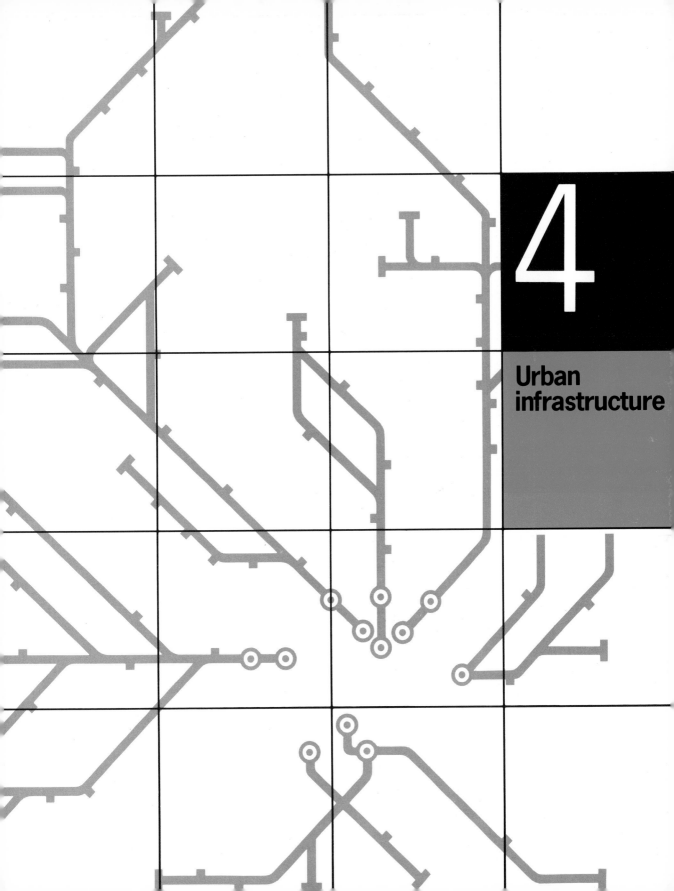

4

Urban
infrastructure

In this chapter the term 'urban infrastructure' is used to cover those aspects of employment and social policies which influence urban development and the quality of life in towns and cities.

Towns wax and wane. They have done so throughout recorded history and doubtless always will. If a town's economy declines, sources of work dry up, people move away and buildings fall empty and decay. Decline can be slow and almost imperceptible to those living there, or it can be shatteringly swift if the town is over-dependent on one source of employment. Some towns can suffer from too much prosperity; economic pressures create sharp stresses—demands for more housing, more shops, more cars and more roads, with a consequent acceleration in land values. But since adequate employment opportunities are vital to the prosperity of all towns and cities, all municipalities strive to ensure stable and diverse employment for their people—never an easy task in times of rapid technological change or economic difficulty. Central government's public expenditure policies and priorities, and particularly investment programmes on housing, roads and urban development, reflect fluctuating national economic fortunes and inevitably impose constraints on the activities of local authorities.

Regional employment policies

A major structural imbalance in the United Kingdom underlies the efforts and activities of individual local authorities to ensure prosperity for their area. In the 19th century the economic centre of gravity of the nation lay in the North of England, in Scotland and in South Wales, being based on the coal, steel, shipbuilding and textile industries. Today these older basic industries are declining and the economic centre of gravity has moved to the South of England. One out of every three people in the United Kingdom now lives in London and the South-East region of England —some 17 million people.

Consequently, throughout the post-war period successive governments have striven to secure a more balanced national distribution of employment by encouraging industry to move to the older industrial areas —the 'assisted areas' or 'Areas for Expansion' as they are now called. This has been done through a system of industrial development certificates (IDCs) and through a range of

financial incentives. The IDC system enables the Government to check on the development of new industrial premises, or the expansion of existing premises, above certain size limits, to see whether the firm concerned would be able and willing to move to an assisted area. Over the years a variety of incentives have emerged to persuade firms to move. These have included providing government factories at low rents; loans and grants towards the cost of new buildings and plant; investment grants towards the cost of production equipment; selective assistance for projects likely to provide employment; assistance towards the retraining of workers and rehousing grants. At the receiving end a hierarchy of assisted areas has developed— Special Development Areas, Development Areas and Intermediate Areas—with different levels of financial inducements.

The present Government have reviewed this regional industrial policy and are making various changes designed to concentrate assistance more discriminately and more selectively on areas with severe economic problems within the overall policy of encouraging national industrial vitality and prosperity throughout the country.

Matching jobs and people was also an important element in the new town and town development schemes launched as part of the planned dispersal of people from the conurbations (see chapter 1). The new towns, particularly, were intended to be self-contained communities and not dormitories for the large cities as had tended to happen with peripheral development during the inter-war years. Potential conflicts with national policies on the redistribution of industry were resolved by giving new towns and new town development schemes outside the assisted areas second priority to the latter in competing for 'footloose' industry. Present policy is still to give first priority to the assisted areas and to give those inner city areas with partnership arrangements (see page 26) greater priority now than the new towns.

Location of industry within towns

Although national policies on the balance of industrial development throughout the country have been remarkably constant throughout the post-war period, there has been an interesting change in policies and attitudes towards the location of industry within urban areas. For some 20 years after the war the basic policy was to segregate industry from residential and other areas in the town. Separate industrial estates were a feature of the master plans of all the early new towns, and equally a feature in the town plans for existing towns. This was the era in which it was taken as axiomatic that 'non-conforming uses'—i.e. activities that did not conform with the main character of the particular area, be it housing, commerce or industry—should be removed. This was a natural reaction to the juxtaposition of industrial and residential areas which characterised the Victorian industrial towns, where mills and factories spread noise, smoke and other forms of pollution over nearby housing.

Nowadays mixed development has become more acceptable. Experience with large segregated industrial estates in towns shows that employees' journeys to work can generate heavy surges of traffic across the town. Modern industry is cleaner and less noisy, and dispersal throughout the urban area could help to spread traffic loads. Of course some industrial plants must be situated outside residential areas for reasons of noise, pollution or safety, or because they generate unacceptably heavy traffic. But others, particularly small firms and small businesses employing local people, can be located near shops or housing without damage to the urban environment. There is now a greater readiness to allow industry to expand in its present location, or near to it, and to consider the possibility of allowing new industrial development on derelict or vacant land. But this is tempered by growing public concern over safety hazards, in particular from the use of toxic materials in some industrial processes and their storage on industrial premises.

The formidable employment problems in the inner areas of the larger cities have already been described in chapter 1. To some extent they result from earlier policies which emphasised the decentralisation of people and jobs from the conurbations and the large-scale clearance of the slums. Many small businesses did not survive the slum clearance and elimination of non-conforming uses; relocation to areas zoned for industry proved too costly or impracticable. Local authorities with inner area problems have now been given special powers to declare 'industrial improvement areas' and provide financial inducements to attract industry back into these areas. Small firms could have a particularly important role in the revitalisation of these decaying areas. Indeed there is now much greater recognition of the importance

of small firms generally in the national economy. Various fiscal and other measures have been adopted to encourage their growth, as potential providers of employment.

Service industries

Employment in service industries has not hitherto presented problems comparable to those in manufacturing industry. There was a boom in service employment, particularly office employment, in the first half of the 1960s when employment in the service industries increased by 1 million people, most of them women and many of them married. This helped to mask the effects of the decline in manufacturing employment in the large towns.

The office boom led the Government of the day to set up a Location of Offices Bureau to encourage dispersal of office development from London to other parts of the country and the succeeding Government to institute a system of 'office development permits' (ODPs) fashioned on the same lines as industrial development certificates. Some dispersal was achieved but mainly to nearby areas or within the South-East region. The Bureau is now being wound up and the ODP system abolished.

The service sector has continued to grow, but at a slower pace since the early 1960s. This is however the sector where employment prospects may be under threat from future developments in communications technology —word processors, electronic mail and other forms of rapid computerised communication, adding to the already complex employment problems facing urban authorities.

Road and rail

Road and rail investment policies have always been closely linked with industrial policies. The country's motorway network, and the improvements to its highway system, have in the main been designed to improve communications links between the major industrial areas, between the industrial areas and the main ports, and between the assisted areas and the rest of the country. Good communications have always been considered an important element in inducing new industries to settle in the assisted areas. Most of the northern conurbations—Manchester, Liverpool, Tyneside and Glasgow—are now well served with a network of motorways or

Planning for work

Patterns of employment play a major part in urban planning. The concentration of economic activity in South East England has been matched by a decline in Britain's traditional centres of industry. Specially designated areas, in which financial incentives are provided for industrial development, have therefore been created with the aim of redistributing employment in a more balanced fashion throughout the country. The map shows the hierarchy of these 'Areas for Expansion' as they will be, subject to review, from 1 August 1982.

Until recently, new industrial developments were invariably segregated from residential and commercial areas. Today, the success of anti-pollution measures and the need to spread traffic loads evenly in towns has made mixed development more acceptable. Buildings such as the Herman Miller factory in Bath, 1, and the Olsen Amenity Building, in Tower Hamlets, London, 2, 3, are designed to blend easily with their surroundings, as well as providing a pleasant working environment for their employees. 4, All the major preoccupations of present-day urban planning are reflected in the London Docklands, an area of 2,225 ha (5,500 acres) affected by London's declining role as a major port. A comprehensive development plan is now under way which aims to blend new and existing industry, housing, commercial, educational and recreational facilities, and road and rail transport.

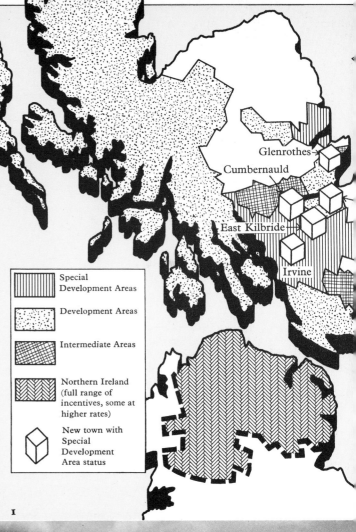

Glenrothes
Cumbernauld
East Kilbride
Irvine

Special Development Areas

Development Areas

Intermediate Areas

Northern Ireland (full range of incentives, some at higher rates)

New town with Special Development Area status

1

Shetland Islands

Orkney Islands

Livingston

Washington
Peterlee

Skelmersdale
Runcorn

London

4

2

3

trunk roads. British Rail electrification schemes and high-speed inter-city rail services have had similar objectives.

Since the mid-1960s environmental considerations have featured increasingly in the composition of the national road programme, not only in the careful choice of routes for new roads so as to minimise environmental effects on the countryside, but also in the increasing number of ring roads and local bypasses constructed to take through traffic out of urban areas. Cities such as Oxford have long had a system of ring roads for this purpose; now many small towns and villages sited across main trunk roads have benefited from the elimination of through traffic.

Within the large cities the problem of reconciling the need for efficient movement of goods and people with environmental needs has proved far more difficult to resolve. During the reconstruction era, in the 1950s and early 1960s, much urban road building took place. Just as the housing subsidy system of that time tended to encourage local authorities to build high-rise blocks of flats, so the central government grant of 75 per cent on the cost of new or improved urban roads proved a powerful incentive to local authorities to concentrate on road building rather than on traffic management schemes and public transport policies. Many new roads were built through the cleared slum areas to link with, and remove traffic from, the city centres, which were also undergoing redevelopment. Ever more elaborate plans were being prepared to build urban ring road systems, to motorway proportions, to cope with growing volumes of urban traffic and to link cities with the inter-urban motorway network, which was also under construction.

The public revolt against the scale, the pace and the damaging effects of these urban road schemes has already been described in chapter 1. Schemes which involved the destruction of fit housing rather than slum housing met with bitter opposition at public inquiries. There was sustained and cogent opposition to the motorway proposals in the Greater London Development Plan, which involved building a 'motorway box' around the inner area of the metropolis and another motorway ring through the suburban areas. The distressing effects on families living alongside newly opened stretches of urban motorways created public concern. The Acklam Road case, in which people had to be moved from houses alongside the Westway motorway in London, polarised public opinion in much the same way as the Ronan Point disaster (see page 56) had done earlier in a different context.

Since the late 1960s there have been organisational, subsidy and policy changes in relation to transport infrastructure. Clearer recognition of the need to integrate land-use, transport and urban environmental policies led to the preparation of major land-use/transport plans. Responsibility for co-ordinating all public transport services has been transferred to specially appointed passenger transport authorities in the larger conurbations. The system of specific road grants has been replaced by a single, comprehensive transport grant which gives local authorities greater freedom to decide how their transport system, including roads, should be developed. They now submit annually to central government a transport policy and programme setting out their strategic aims together with a five-year programme to achieve them. This programme is rolled forward annually. It covers roads, public transport policies, traffic management and parking policies and policies for lorry routes—a subject which remains highly contentious.

Some authorities have embarked on major changes in their transport infrastructure, examples being the urban transport plan adopted by Liverpool and the mass transit system instituted by Tyneside. The Tyneside Metro is a rapid transport system using electrically driven 'metrocars' on a track separated from other traffic. It is designed to remedy traffic congestion and other problems which beset the area. In 1973 the Tyneside Metropolitan Railway Bill received the Royal Assent and, with 70 per cent of the money coming from central government, work on the project began. The final network makes use of long stretches of existing railway and will comprise 41 stations, 4 miles of underground route, a bridge over the Tyne and a viaduct. It is designed to carry 20,000 passengers an hour in each direction, passenger and train movements being monitored on closed-circuit television linked to a control centre. Buses from outlying areas will serve the Metro interchanges whilst those buses whose routes do not go close to the Metro will enjoy priority in reaching Tyneside. Motorists will be able to park and pick up or set down passengers at interchanges. It is due to be operational in the early 1980s.

Nowadays urban road building is largely confined to small-scale, incremental improvements to the existing road system. Comprehensive traffic management schemes have proved that it is possible to cope with greater volumes of traffic without unacceptable congestion than had been envisaged previously. These schemes serve a variety of purposes. There are schemes to eliminate or reduce traffic in city centres and schemes which can improve access to industrial and commercial premises. Local authorities have been asked to take full account of the extra costs likely to be placed on industry when appraising proposals for re-routeing commercial vehicles and to bear in mind that industrial transport costs can often be reduced if firms are sited with convenient access to existing motorway or trunk roads or railway lines. In their policies for the levels of public transport services, and the fares to be charged, local authorities have been asked to pay regard to the need to cater adequately for journeys to work when shifts in population or industry have separated people from their places of work. Traffic management can be a significant instrument in reinforcing wider urban objectives.

Social policies

Until the early 1960s town-planning policies tended to develop independently from national policies on education, poverty, unemployment and other aspects of a welfare society. It was assumed that a clean, new and pleasant physical environment, carefully planned and executed, would be sufficient in itself—a philosophy which had roots going back to the activities of Victorian philanthropists who built 'model' housing estates for their workers.

It was not that post-war town planning ignored community needs. Indeed, the planners' thinking revolved around the concept of the 'neighbourhood', which found its clearest expression in the green-field new town and town development schemes. The basic urban unit was a residential area of about 6–10,000 people provided with a small neighbourhood shopping centre and some corner shops. There were primary schools within walking distance for the younger children and secondary schools within cycling distance for the older children, a planned ratio of children's play spaces and neighbourhood playing fields, and a community hall, church and public house. The whole neighbourhood was carefully segregated from industrial premises and surrounded by roads which ensured that through traffic was excluded from the housing area. Many of these schemes, once landscaped and mellowed with time, have proved to be pleasant and acceptable environments for their inhabitants.

On the other hand some of the social problems now facing urban authorities result from the scale and pace of post-war reconstruction. In the United Kingdom there is a strong preference for low-density, low-rise housing; the construction of tower blocks proved universally unpopular, and other high-density housing, five to six storeys high, often in large connected blocks, has proved only slightly less so. Building large numbers of new houses quickly threatened to overwhelm local authority housing management systems. Urban authorities had to cope with new types of housing, some with inherent management problems and a population that had been uprooted. The decline of the private rented housing sector and the expansion of the public rented sector also resulted in local authorities having to absorb more disadvantaged tenants such as poor families, homeless members of broken families, single parents, etc.

As a result the local authority sector has tended to become the landlord of last resort. Within it there is now a much greater variety of housing. Tenants seek transfers to more desirable housing stock and the polarisation of 'good' and 'bad' housing estates is becoming more noticeable. Overstretched management and maintenance services find it difficult to cope with the demands of high-density estates and with concentrations of disadvantaged families. This can lead to a downward spiral of neglect and low morale, in which housing proves difficult to let even though it has been built since the war.

Investigation into the problems of 'difficult-to-let' estates has resulted in a new concern to lower abnormally high densities of children in these estates, which appear statistically related to the incidence of vandalism. There is a fresh emphasis on the importance of a 'global' approach in tackling run-down estates, whereby improvements in local housing management are integrated and coordinated with lettings, maintenance, refuse collection, policing, landscaping and other activities. A key feature is the full involvement of, and consultation with, residents as an essential part in raising morale, safeguarding improvements and ensuring that the priorities for action are right. Experimental work is taking place under the aegis of the Department of the Environment in two estates—one in Hackney, London, and the other in Bolton, Lancashire.

Transport

1

more efficient urban and inter-urban transport. In Runcorn New Town, a Busway segregated from other traffic, 1, ensures rapid transit between the residential areas and other parts of the town. The M62 is one of Britain's most recent motorway developments. The 11½ mile stretch connecting the M1 and the A1 near Ferrybridge, West Yorkshire, 2, was opened in 1974.

The dispersal of population from cities, large-scale redevelopment and the relocation of industry all increase the need for efficient transport systems. In Britain in recent years, much emphasis has been laid on the development of faster,

2

Two new city metro systems have recently been put into commission. The Glasgow Metro, 3, was opened to the public in April 1980. The Tyne and Wear Metro, 4,5, opened to the public in August 1980, will by the time of its completion in 1983 consist of 34 miles of track servicing 41 stations.

The 250 km/h (156 mph) Advanced Passenger Train, 6, due to come into service in October, reduces the journey time between London and Glasgow from five to just over four hours.

3

4

6

5

Various strands in urban planning and social policies began to merge in the 1960s. The problems of the inner areas of the larger cities proved to be the catalyst. There had been an influx of immigration into the old and deteriorating housing in inner city areas which had escaped slum clearance. Problems of race, custom and education compounded the problems created by the dispersal of people and jobs from these inner areas and the lack of employment opportunities suitable for the skills of the remaining inhabitants. As described in chapter 1, policies of positive discrimination on an area basis developed first in the educational field, then in housing. The important inner area studies in London, Birmingham and Liverpool (see page 26) unravelled the full complexity of the problems in these inner areas and led to the Inner Urban Areas Act of 1978.

Today there is a clearer understanding that the built environment, the economic environment and the social environment are indivisible. Town-planning policies, housing and transport policies, economic and social policies, conservation and rehabilitation policies, anti-pollution and many other policies, not least expenditure policies, all interact and at times conflict with each other. Urban renewal is now increasingly recognised as being an immensely complex task requiring an amalgam of carefully co-ordinated actions in many different fields if the mistakes of the past are not to be repeated and the problems of the future are to be tackled effectively.

5

Public participation

Pressures for more effective public involvement in the decisions and activities of all public authorities have grown steadily as the ambit of State activity has expanded. Urban policies have been no exception to this general trend. As is well known, the 'Englishman's home is his castle'. Anything that impinges on the relationship between the individual and authority and the delicate balance between private rights and public advantage, particularly if it affects land or property, always arouses interest and emotions.

In this report the term 'public participation' is used to cover not only the procedural processes by which individuals, or groups of individuals, have an opportunity to influence decisions by public authorities on town planning policies and development proposals, but also the policies which foster community involvement in urban environmental affairs through actions as well as comment.

The public inquiry

Until the 1960s there was little public pressure for participation in the decision-making processes of town planning. In the main this reflected a wide consensus on the main urban planning objectives as being to disperse people and jobs from over-crowded cities to decent new environments; to get on with the rebuilding of those cities, yet still contain them with green belts; and to deal with a national housing shortage and the legacy of urban obsolescence.

Initially, public authorities advertised their urban plans and proposals, and objections and representations on them were aired through the mechanism of the 'public local inquiry'. This mechanism applied, and to a large extent still applies, throughout the town-planning field, for development plans; for proposals to acquire compulsorily land and buildings for roads, schools, housing or any other urban purpose; for slum clearance; for the designation of sites for a new town; and of course for planning applications by developers which raise matters of public interest.

The procedure is essentially simple. An Inspector appointed by the relevant Minister hears and reports on the proposals in question and the objections and representations made . about them. After considering the Inspector's report and recommendations the Minister issues his decision (in certain categories of planning applications this is delegated to the Inspector without further reference to the Minister). These decisions are final, and there is no right of appeal against their substance. There is a right to challenge the validity of the decision in the courts on purely procedural points within a limited period—generally six weeks.

Until the late 1970s, public reaction to planning policies and decisions focussed on these public inquiry procedures, to ensure that they were fair and impartial, and were seen to be so. It was not that public opinion was indifferent to town planning. As early as 1947 there was strong local opposition to the designation orders delimiting the sites of the first new towns. Litigation occurred for example over the designation order for Stevenage. This opposition arose not only from the natural repugnance of inhabitants in a small settlement to having a large town built around them, but also from the fact that designation made all the land within the designated area liable to compulsory acquisition. Significantly there was the feeling that this was the Minister's own order, the inquiry was being conducted by one of his own Inspectors, and he was therefore being judge and jury in his own case. The objectors succeeded in having the Stevenage designation order quashed in the High Court, but this decision was reversed by the Court of Appeal and the reversal was upheld in the House of Lords. The Court ruled that the process of designation was an administrative one, and not quasi-judicial as pertained in other public inquiries held to consider, for example, disputes between a local authority and a developer over a particular planning application.

There was also lively public interest in some of the early development plans prepared by the local planning authorities—the first statutory development plan for London attracted over 7,000 objections in the mid-1950s.

In 1957 a wide-ranging report on administrative tribunals and inquiries (the Franks Report) explicitly stated that the operations of tribunals and inquiries should be characterised by 'openness, fairness and impartiality' and went on to say:
'Here we need give only brief examples of their application. Take openness. If these procedures were wholly secret the basis of confidence and acceptability would be lacking. Next take fairness. If the objector were not allowed to state his case there would be nothing to stop oppression. Thirdly there is impartiality. How can a citizen be

satisfied unless he feels that those who decide his case come to their decision with open minds?'

Subsequently a Council of Tribunals was set up and public inquiry procedures on town-planning matters were made more explicit and codified. They now involve amongst many other things, re-opening inquiries to consider fresh evidence and the publication of Inspectors' reports with fully reasoned decision letters. These procedures have ensured scrupulous regard for the principles of openness, fairness and impartiality. Inevitably, procedures have lengthened and with them the time-scale of decision-making. This was one of the reasons (but not the only one) why the development plans of the 1950s fell out of step with the surge of redevelopment then taking place.

Public participation in town planning

Pressure for more public participation in the planning processes arose in the 1960s and reflected the atmosphere of the time. People were concerned about the quality of the new development and its social effects. The more grandiose and ambitious plans for re-shaping cities were out of tune with new public attitudes. There were sharp changes in public opinion which led to the switch from massive redevelopment to conservation and gradual renewal. People wanted more say in the decisions which were shaping their urban environment and there was far greater awareness of environmental matters in all their manifestations. The era of 'public participation' had arrived.

Following a review of the whole development plan system in the mid-1960s, a Town and Country Planning Act passed in 1968 inaugurated the new arrangements—centrally approved broad 'structure plans' and locally approved detailed 'local plans'. Significantly, the Act placed a statutory duty on local planning authorities to consult the public when both structure plans and local plans were being prepared. This was an important step forward in additional public involvement in the planning processes which in no way prevented individuals or organisations from objecting to the final proposals published in the plans.

It has been left to individual local authorities to work out how best to develop systems of public participation in this context. General guidance on the subject was given in a government report published in 1969 under the title *People and planning* (the Skeffington Report). It recommended that the public should be kept informed throughout the preparation of the plan, that they should be encouraged to participate in the surveys on which the plan was to be based and to comment on the draft plan and alternative possibilities, and that they should subsequently be told by the local authority how far it had been possible to adjust the plan to take account of the views expressed. Guidance was also given on the use of various techniques such as meetings, exhibitions, leaflets and local radio and press facilities. Further advice was given to local authorities some years later, stressing the importance of giving the public opportunities of expressing its views before approval was given to proposals which were of wide concern or likely to have a substantial impact on the environment.

Although there is a distinction between constructive participation in the preparation of plans, and objections to completed plans or planning applications, results to date have been varied. In some cases the participation processes have indicated a general consensus over the policies suggested, but more often they have served to highlight conflict. Although some local authorities have been more successful than others in involving the public in the preparation of their plans, all are finding it to be a time-consuming and increasingly costly process.

This is not surprising. Public participation in town planning is one of those deceptively simple concepts which bristle with difficulties. For example, how can the public participation processes be best reconciled with democratic control of central and local administration? Electoral processes alone do not serve the purposes of participation. But if elected representatives are by-passed there is a danger that these processes could undermine democratic political control of public decision-making. They must therefore be clearly incorporated into the existing local government systems. In this context the Secretary of State for the Environment has recently said:
'I do not want to reduce the opportunity that people have to stand up for their rights. But I want them to have those opportunities within a structured system. I want them to be able to feel that their views are taken on board and quickly. And I want them to understand that at the end of the day the responsibility of the locally elected authority is to reconcile whatever

Planning
participation and protest

Throughout the post-war period, public participation in urban planning has been possible through the medium of the public inquiry. Since the early 1960s, however, public awareness of the need for participation has increased, and public protest has become a common method of expressing opposition to official views and decisions.

The steps in the progress of a planning application for a specific development are shown in the diagram.

1,2, Publicity material issued by local authorities in Essex and West Midlands to encourage public participation in structure plans.

The disruptive effects of urban motorway building have aroused considerable public disapproval.

3, Members of the public objecting to the building of the M25 motorway in Kent applaud an unofficial speaker at the public inquiry in September 1978.

Consultations are carried out with other council departments and, often, with neighbouring authorities, Dept. of Environment, British Rail, etc. Householders likely to be affected by the development are notified.

All applications must satisfy certain standards and planning requirements. These range from the size and appearance of buildings, the materials in use, to the effect on existing social amenities of a building and its users.

All observations and comments made by interested parties are collected and considered in relation to the application.

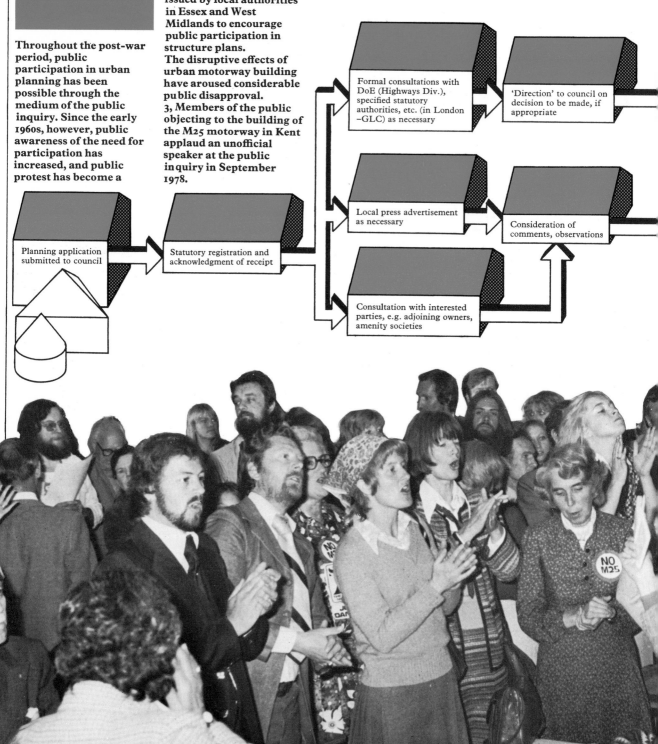

Planning application submitted to council

Statutory registration and acknowledgment of receipt

Formal consultations with DoE (Highways Div.), specified statutory authorities, etc. (in London –GLC) as necessary

'Direction' to council on decision to be made, if appropriate

Local press advertisement as necessary

Consultation with interested parties, e.g. adjoining owners, amenity societies

Consideration of comments, observations

The application is now assessed in the light of all the available information. Often the council will ask the applicant to modify his plans to satisfy a specific objection or to comply with planning standards.

A recommendation to grant or refuse the application is made to the committee. To help speed the process the planning officer may have authority to approve or refuse certain types of application without reference to the committee.

The planning committee may consist of 15 to 25 councillors and will meet every 4 weeks or so. They may refuse an application, or approve it subject or not to the applicant fulfilling certain conditions.

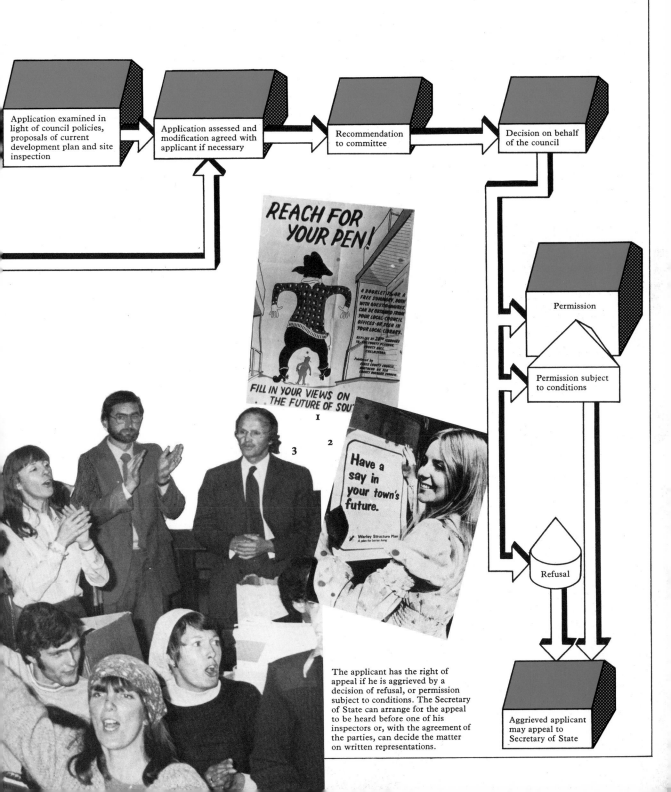

Application examined in light of council policies, proposals of current development plan and site inspection

Application assessed and modification agreed with applicant if necessary

Recommendation to committee

Decision on behalf of the council

REACH FOR YOUR PEN!

FILL IN YOUR VIEWS ON THE FUTURE OF SOUT

Have a say in your town's future.

Warley Structure Plan
A plan for better living

Permission

Permission subject to conditions

Refusal

The applicant has the right of appeal if he is aggrieved by a decision of refusal, or permission subject to conditions. The Secretary of State can arrange for the appeal to be heard before one of his inspectors or, with the agreement of the parties, can decide the matter on written representations.

Aggrieved applicant may appeal to Secretary of State

conflicts have emerged.'

Where is the balance to be drawn between the value of public participation and its time and cost, and how are decisions, when finally taken, going to be made to 'stick' and not be subject to repeated reassessments and endless controversy? Public participation can be of great value if it produces information and views contributing to better decisions and policies, and public consent for, and commitment to, those decisions and policies. It is of less value if the processes become unduly prolonged and the broad public interest is obscured by small, highly vocal minorities objecting strongly to particular features in the plan.

How is the 'silent majority' to be persuaded to participate so that plans and policies are not unduly influenced by a few pressure groups? It is the most natural thing in the world to complain over policies that are disliked but otherwise not to bother. Even the capacity of individuals or groups to participate may be severely tested when it comes to mastering, in leisure hours, the complex and interlocking issues involved in major plans so that constructive comments can be made. The task can often strain the resources even of national interest groups, which are usually equipped with full-time staff and have access to highly professional advice.

Then there is the problem of 'blight'. There can be a conflict between the need to give full publicity at an early stage to certain proposals in order to stimulate public discussion and the fact that they may cause hardship to individuals by their blighting effect on land and property, even though some of them may never materialise. The publication of alternative lines for road proposals is a notable example.

These and other problems inherent in the concept of public participation have yet to be satisfactorily resolved. There is always a danger that the spirit behind the concept of participation might be lost in processes which become too ritualised and institutionalised; continued experimentation in methods, techniques and objectives seems essential.

One interesting development has been the institution of the 'examination in public' (EIP) as a procedure for considering the proposals in structure plans. These plans deal with broad strategies and broad policies for the area concerned; they do not indicate the effect of those policies on individual properties and property rights. The EIP provides the Secretary of State with the information and arguments which he needs, in addition to the material in the plan itself and the comments, objections and representations on it, so as to enable him to reach a decision on the plan. It is conducted by a small panel appointed by the Secretary of State and deals only with selected issues and not with every comment or objection made to the plan. It is conducted with selected participants—the composition of the groups changing with each issue under discussion—and proceedings take the form of an informal, probing discussion led by the panel rather than the more formal adversarial techniques used in public inquiries.

This new system presupposes that there has been extensive public participation prior to submission of the plan for ministerial approval. But it also recognises that not enough attention has been paid in the past to the need for reasonable speed in considering and deciding on development plans or to the costs of delay, including prolonged uncertainty and blight. It has resulted in a noticeable reduction in the length of time taken to consider the main issues involved—they can often be reduced to a few weeks rather than the many months involved in traditional public inquiries—and has proved an interesting and worthwhile form of public participation.

Community involvement

Nowadays public participation policies are moving beyond arrangements and procedures designed to elicit and evaluate public reactions to urban plans in their early stages. They are moving into the much more complex and difficult field of encouraging civic participation by activity rather than words—constructive action by individuals or small local groups aimed at improving their own local urban environment rather than simply commenting on the plans of the public authority.

The 'partnership' schemes now operating in the inner areas of the large cities (see page 26) are pointing the way to a more constructive form of public participation in the urban environment. These schemes involve joint action by central and local government, employers and trade unions and a host of voluntary bodies, all operating with the common aim of improving the distressing conditions prevalent in the inner areas. They are opening up new lines of communication between these bodies, and helping to foster the sense of self-reliance and of pride in achievement which are likely to be crucial to their success.

An interesting example of mutual self-help and co-operation are the 'enterprise agencies' being developed in London, Birmingham, Manchester and some of the other large cities. Each agency is a consortium of large firms, banks and the local chamber of commerce which aims to help small businesses with their financial, technical and other problems and to help in the regeneration of inner city areas.

The active involvement of trade councils schools and other groups in the 'quiet town' experiment in Darlington has already been described (see page 43). Another interesting exercise in community participation has been launched recently in the Greater Manchester area. Called Impact, it is a campaign sponsored by the Greater Manchester County Council to stimulate improvements, large or small, to the urban environment by enlisting the aid of everyone concerned—householders, shopkeepers, businesses, industrialists and community groups. The aim is to make an impact on the local environment through a wide variety of measures such as cleaning up derelict areas, planting flowers and shrubs in homes or places of work and organising collections for recycling bottles and paper.

The Woodlands area in Glasgow provides another example of community involvement —in this case aimed at arresting the decline of a housing area. Woodlands is a well-defined triangle of 23 tenement blocks about 90 years old situated in the inner city area of Glasgow. At the beginning of the 1970s this area had so deteriorated that it had an anticipated life of only five to seven years. However, local residents used the environmental grants available under the Housing (Scotland) Act of 1969 as a means of reversing the area's decline. They drew up plans for cleaning and restoring the external appearance of the buildings and rear courts. The work has been eminently successful; with the help of the local authority in landscaping and traffic-management measures, streets lined with dark, soot-stained façades have been converted into bright, attractive avenues. A lively community spirit has both survived and flourished.

In one sense the development of housing associations and housing societies represents a form of community participation in urban matters. They have been called the 'third arm' on the housing front, complementing the activities of local authorities and the private sector. They operate on a non-profit-making basis and generally aim to fill the gap left by the diminishing numbers of private landlords, particularly in areas of housing stress. They play a variety of roles, helping to meet housing needs (including catering for the elderly and the handicapped), providing small-scale and less remote housing management than that provided by local authorities, and experimenting with forms of tenant participation. There are a variety of associations, ranging from those offering conventional tenancies to co-ownership schemes, from those offering specialised housing to others that are more diverse, and from large associations to very small. Today there are over 2,700 of these associations.

Successive governments have long sought to increase home ownership. In the 25 years between 1951 and 1976 the proportion of owner-occupied dwellings has risen from 31 per cent to 55 per cent of the total housing stock in England and Wales. The present Government has introduced legislation to give council house tenants a right to purchase their house—a matter of current political controversy. Home ownership provides a natural stimulus to improve and maintain property. It can also provide an impetus towards creative interest in local environmental care and maintenance.

Despite the great increase in home ownership there are still some millions of households living in public-sector rented accommodation, many of whom neither wish, or are able, to afford home ownership. Policies are being developed to create a 'tenant's charter' in order to safeguard and extend tenants' rights and to free them from unnecessarily restrictive housing management practices. Local housing authorities are being encouraged to seek greater tenant involvement in housing management, including the development of housing management cooperatives. The example of tenant involvement in actions to deal with the social problems in difficult-to-let and run-down housing estates has already been described in chapter 4 (see page 71).

Finally, but by no means least, there are all the activities of numerous local amenity societies operating under the general umbrella of the Civic Trust, which have been active in a variety of ways in the conservation movement—in schemes for improving and 'face-lifting' the urban environment and in activities which have for example helped to highlight the problem of urban 'wasteland'. Small-scale and sensitive

Community action

Outside the framework of official planning processes there is ample scope for community activities which make a more immediate impact on the urban environment. In one of the most notable recent examples of community action, residents of a late Victorian tenement block in the Woodlands area of Glasgow embarked on a 'clean-up' campaign with the help of grants from the Glasgow District Council. The successful scheme was eventually extended to 23 tenement blocks in the area and involved stone-cleaning, renovation of the back courts, new street furniture and tree-planting, and an extensive traffic management scheme.

1, Mrs Dorothy Henderson, one of the founders of the scheme and chairman of the Woodlands Residents' Association, in front of one of the renovated tenements.

2,3, Back yards in the Woodlands area before and after improvement. Launched in July 1979, the Impact scheme sponsored by the Greater Manchester County Council aims to involve

I've made an
impact
improvement
action

4

impact news

Tree Week in Salford

MAKE AN IMPACT IN THE 80's

Having a Smashing Time at Wigan Pier

5

6

Two different forms of community involvement in environmental measures: 7,8, The Westminster City Council's campaign to clean up central London relies on sponsorship from local tradesmen and companies, trade associations, consumer groups and public bodies. 9, The City Farm Movement aims to set up projects involving animals and gardening on plots of urban wasteland in towns and cities throughout Britain. There are some 30 City Farms now in existence.

as many different sectors of the community as possible in a widely varied programme of environmental improvements. An extensive publicity campaign has been instituted, including lapel stickers, 4, a newspaper, 5, and a special bus, 6.

CITY FARMS

Using Wasteland in Towns And Cities For Mutual-Help Projects Involving Gardening And Farm Animals

Inter-Action's City Farm Advisory Service is free of charge to community groups and individuals helping to start programmes of social benefit renovation of old buildings has encouraged individuals and organisations to conserve and enhance local environments, and has generally helped to foster a widening interest in the quality of urban life.

To conclude, conflict is inherent in much of town planning—conflict between public advantage and private interests, between public authorities, developers and special interest groups. It is important that these conflicts should be recognised and given full expression in a systematic way before decisions are finally taken by those responsible.

The mechanism of the public local inquiry is a vital protection. It is important that its procedures should be governed by the principles of 'openness, fairness and impartiality' if public respect for the procedure is to be maintained.

It is also important that the public are given effective opportunities to comment on urban plans and policies at an early stage in their formulation. The statutory provision for consultation on structure and local plans in the 1968 Town and Country Planning Act is a milestone in this respect. But experience shows that there are formidable problems in this process, not least the cost and time involved and the difficulties of eliciting views from the silent majority. Continued experimentation in techniques and methods is essential.

Public participation by consultation, comment and disputation is not, however, enough. Participation by community involvement and creative activity is likely to be more effective and fruitful in the longer term. This approach may be more fitted to the urban problems of the 1980s, as we move from large-scale and socially destructive redevelopment and indiscriminate preservation to an urban renewal policy which is more balanced, small-scale, sensitive and gradual. A creative, 'grass-roots' form of community participation which harnesses the energies of people living in cities could be an essential component of success in making towns and cities better places in which to live.

6

The role of local authorities

GMC

The local government system

The United Kingdom has a long-established system of democratically elected local authorities with a strong tradition of independence. The main responsibility for town and country planning, including urban planning and other related policies such as housing etc., rests mainly with local government, which operates within a statutory framework laid down by Parliament and administrative and policy guidelines set by central government. Other agencies dealing with water, health and employment operate outside the local authority structure.

The 1970s saw a major reorganisation of local government, which had remained basically unchanged since the 19th century. In England and Wales a new system came into operation in 1974. Outside London, the number of authorities was reduced from 1,390 to 422. (Local government in London had been reorganised in 1965, when the Greater London Council was set up with responsibilities, amongst other things, for strategic planning and transportation for the whole of the Greater London area. Thirty-two London borough councils and the City of London had responsibility for local planning and the control of development.)

The new local government pattern consists of six metropolitan counties for the conurbations and 47 non-metropolitan counties elsewhere. Within these counties there are 36 metropolitan district councils and 333 non-metropolitan district councils covering much larger areas than the former, more numerous authorities. The reorganisation has had the effect of bringing together for the first time under one strategic authority separate towns that had merged into conurbations such as the West Midlands area and Greater Manchester, each with a population of over 2·5 million, the West Yorkshire conurbation with 1 million and Merseyside with over 1·5 million.

The county councils are the strategic planning authorities responsible for the preparation of structure plans and are also the transportation authorities. The district councils are responsible for the preparation of local plans and for most of the day-to-day control over development. There are complicated arrangements for the division of responsibility on planning matters between these two tiers of authorities, which can lead to delays and duplication. Consequently the present Government has announced proposals designed to clarify the respective roles of county and district councils. In future it is proposed that, except for a few types of specialised development, development control matters will be entirely the responsibility of the district councils.

In Scotland, the new pattern of local government was established in 1975. This provided for nine regional councils, 53 district councils and three new island councils for Orkney, Shetland and the Western Isles, each with comprehensive functions. Unlike in England and Wales, water and sewerage responsibilities are handled by the regional councils and not by separate water authorities, and the three rural regions and the island councils handle all statutory planning matters.

In Northern Ireland, since 1973, the Department of the Environment for Northern Ireland has been the authority which directly administers planning, roads and water supply. Appointed area boards administer health and education services, and the Northern Ireland Housing Executive is the housing authority. There are 26 district councils which are responsible for a limited range of services such as recreation and public health. They nominate members to the area boards and are consulted by the central Departments in the exercise of their functions.

Local authorities have a critical and key role in urban renewal. They are in effect the urban 'managers' (and for that matter also the rural managers where local authority boundaries cross both town and country areas). The way in which the local leadership use their powers does much to set the tone of the urban environment in the town concerned.

Over the years local authorities have been given a wide armoury of statutory powers, duties and responsibilities with implications for urban planning. These do not only cover the preparation of development plans and the exercise of development control. There are byelaw powers controlling the detailed design and construction of buildings; powers to acquire land for a range of purposes; to build new houses and stimulate the improvement and rehabilitation of older houses; to designate conservation areas; to control atmospheric pollution, noise and other forms of pollution; to adopt traffic management and parking measures; to provide schools, libraries and a wide range of personal social services; to dispose of refuse; to clean streets and see that they are adequately lit—in short to provide many of the services which together help to make for civilised urban living.

The role of central government

The responsibilities of central government are less direct but nevertheless important. Central government lays down national policies and priorities for particular services and functions; it also exercises appellate functions where local authority actions affect the rights of other parties, and generally controls local government investment in accordance with the public expenditure policies of the Government of the day.

National policy is expressed in legislation passed through Parliament; it is interpreted in administrative 'circulars' to local authorities (most of which are on sale to the public) and is further amplified in technical advice in bulletins and other documents. The Department of the Environment and its predecessor the old Ministry of Housing and Local Government has, for example, over the years issued bulletins on a wide variety of housing matters. They have produced guidance notes on development control and on issues such as control over the design of buildings, out-of-town shopping centres, etc., and have published bulletins on various aspects of urban renewal.

Central government exercises its appellate functions through the right of 'appeal' to Ministers by individuals affected by the decisions of local authorities. This is particularly so on proposals to acquire compulsorily land and property. In the United Kingdom these powers are confined to public authorities—local authorities, nationalised industries and quasi-governmental bodies such as new town development corporations. The exercise of these powers in the form of compulsory purchase orders (CPOs) requires confirmation by the appropriate Minister in central government, often after a public inquiry has been held to hear the views of objectors. Similarly there are appeals to the Minister against local authority decisions on planning applications.

Many of the legislative codes provide for central government approval of various actions. The Government have recently reviewed the whole range of central government controls over local authorities and it is proposed to repeal or modify some 300 of these. The aim is to allow local authorities, as democratically elected bodies, to be free to get on with the tasks entrusted to them by Parliament without constant intervention in matters of detail from central government. Provisions which allow third parties to appeal to Ministers are, however, retained. This is considered to be the most efficient way, consistent with natural justice, of enabling a third party to have his case considered on its merits without time-consuming and costly reference to the courts.

Central government pays for just over 60 per cent of local authority expenditure, unlike some American cities which have to pay for municipal services out of local revenues. This is done mainly through a block grant, using a complicated formula expressed in terms of 'needs' and 'resources' which is designed to allocate funds in such a way that the poorer local authorities with low rateable resources can nevertheless provide services commensurate with their needs. The details of these arrangements are currently under review. Otherwise local authorities must find the money needed from the 'rates'—a levy on property owners living or operating in the local authority area—or from revenues from their trading services.

The relationship between central and local government is subtle and complex. Rather than that of a principal operating through agents, it is broadly a partnership between two bodies each with their own important responsibilities, one on a national and the other on a local scale.

Urban management

Within this general framework local authorities are now increasingly recognised as having a key role as urban managers. This has not always been so. Urban authorities have often been seen by the public as simply purveyors and operators of a collection of separate services. Many local authorities have traditionally viewed their role in a similar manner. Since the 1960s, however, there has been a growing awareness of the complexity of urban problems and recognition that these problems do not always fit neatly and easily within the scope of one local authority service. With the economic, cultural and physical well-being of the community to consider, urban authorities have been adapting their internal management structures and committee systems to provide for a wider-ranging corporate outlook to their responsibilities.

As urban managers, local authorities now guide, co-ordinate, initiate and control. At one end of this spectrum of activities there may be a local plan for the area which sets out the authority's proposals for development and change over the next 10 years covering housing, employment, traffic and a range of environmental policies. These proposals are subject to public participation, and to public inquiry if there are sustained objections. The Inspector, although appointed by central government, reports to the local authority, who consider his report and decide to what extent they wish to amend their proposals. Provided the local plan conforms with the approved structure plan for the county council area, it can be adopted by the local authority without further ministerial approval.

It has taken some time to change over from the old development plan system to the newer structure/local plan system initiated in the 1968 Town and Country Planning Act, with its new and inevitably lengthy processes of public participation. Local plans are only now coming on stream, and it is too soon to say whether they will prove sufficiently flexible and responsive to continually changing circumstances to be effective guides to urban renewal. There is the danger that lengthy procedures, or tardy revision, could result in their becoming out-dated, as happened with the earlier development plan system in the 1950s and 1960s.

Under the same planning legislation the local authority may also define 'action areas'. These are areas where comprehensive treatment—either redevelopment, rehabilitation or conservation—is proposed. They carry a commitment to start action, and to find the necessary funds, within a 10-year period.

One example is the Covent Garden Action Area instituted by the Greater London Council in 1978. It covers the area vacated by the wholesale fruit, vegetable and flower markets when, after 300 years of trading in Covent Garden, these markets moved to Nine Elms south of the Thames. The existing historic urban fabric is being restored and rehabilitated for commercial, special industrial and residential uses with the aim of bringing new life and economic activity to the area. It is already developing into a lively and attractive neighbourhood with a mixture of trades chosen for their unusual or specialised nature. The whole area focusses on a square originally designed by Inigo Jones in the 1630s. A new London Transport Museum has recently been opened in the former Covent Garden Flower Market in one corner of the square. A vacant site adjoining the former Floral Hall and temporarily used as a community garden is later to be used for an extension to the Royal Opera House. New housing is being provided and older housing improved; the aim is to double the present residential population of 3,000 whilst providing a better environment and better services for residents.

At the opposite end of the urban management spectrum there are the local authority's decisions on individual applications for planning permission for development. These can range from an application to extend a single house to proposals for a large new housing estate or a major shopping/office/housing complex. They are dealt with by the well established development control procedures which have been operating since the 1947 Town and Country Planning Act. But this detailed development control is essentially a negative function. It prevents undesirable development in unsuitable places, but it does not in itself promote development. This latter function depends on the activities of others, which in turn reflect the pressures for change operating in the area. There may be too few applications in places where the local authority would welcome development, or too many in the wrong places. An increasing number of authorities are using the technique of the 'developer's brief'—a document which sets out the local authority's ideas on the type and scale of development that would be acceptable for certain important or sensitive areas.

In the middle of the spectrum of urban management activities there are many actions and initiatives which can be undertaken by local authorities. They can build houses for those in special need, offer improvement grants for older housing, or mortgages for house purchase. They can re-route traffic, make parking arrangements, and carry out environmental measures to smarten up areas and promote the right atmosphere for private investment and private development. They can designate smoke control areas, conservation areas, noise abatement zones, housing improvement areas and housing action areas, although the sheer multiplicity of these areas can create problems in the co-ordination of local authority services and the deployment of scarce resources.

2

3

1

The closure of the old flower and vegetable markets in Covent Garden in 1974 represented a major opportunity for London's planners. A market had been held in the central Piazza for over 300 years and the area had a wealth of historical associations, a large number of fine buildings, and a unique character derived from the life of the market and its many restaurants, pubs and theatres. An existing conservation area was extended in 1974, and a comprehensive development scheme instituted which aimed to preserve the area's historic fabric while importing into it new life and commercial activity. Measures have ranged from the regulation of shop-fronts to the encouragement of unusual or specialised businesses. The centre-piece is the main market building in the Piazza, now a pedestrian precinct, which was re-opened in June 1980 as a shopping and entertainment centre.

1, The Piazza, designed by Inigo Jones in 1630, before the building of the central market. 2, The Piazza after the addition of Charles Fowler's market building in 1828. Cast iron and glass canopies were added between the central arcade and the flanking buildings in 1874 and 1888. 3, The restored market building after its opening in June 1980, as commemorated on a poster issued by the GLC.

The dominant features of the restored market building are the two covered courts and the central arcade. The court on the south side of the Piazza has been excavated to create a second storey. Both the courts and the arcade are flanked by specialised shops and cafés and bars. There is an open air restaurant in the northern court, 4.

The planners have attempted to recreate something of the colour and animation which have characterised the market area over the years. 5, A familiar scene at a fruit and vegetable stall in the restored market. 6, Russell Street, looking west towards the Piazza in the early 1900s. 7, Market activity around the portico of St Paul's Church in the early 1970s. 8, The old flower market in the south-east corner of the Piazza has been transformed into a new museum housing London Transport's collection of historic buses and underground trains.

8

4

5

7

Sites due for redevelopment have been put to good temporary use as gardens: The 'Japanese garden' on the Odhams site at the end of Long Acre, 9, has now given way to a new housing development, 10.

9

The Covent Garden area owes much of its character to its fine 18th and 19th century buildings, many of which have historical associations. They are now being restored and maintained to a high standard. Among them are the office buildings on the corner of Garrick Street and King Street, 11, and on the corner of Henrietta Street and Bedford Street, 12.

11

12

10

Not surprisingly, local authority actions are often geared to creating new employment or stabilising existing employment opportunities. These initiatives include setting up special units, or appointments, within the local authority with the prime task of facilitating new industrial or commercial development, an example being the London Industrial Centre created by the Greater London Council. Less common is the creation of an Industrial Capacity Register recording the type of work undertaken by local firms, which can be used by suppliers and contractors. Research in Liverpool showed that many firms had spare capacity for production but lacked the marketing knowledge to obtain orders from other than traditional sources.

The most common approach, however, is for the local authority to make available fully serviced sites for industrial or commercial development. The power to assemble land for development by agreement, or if necessary by compulsion, is an important element in the local authority's armoury. This was used to considerable effect, in partnership with the private sector, in the renewal of many town centres in the 1960s. The local authority assembled the land, leased it to developers and made arrangements to share in the resulting equity. These arrangements were often quite complicated to ensure that civic needs were met.

Certain local authorities have been given special powers in the Inner Urban Areas Act of 1978 to deal with decaying inner areas in selected cities. The basic aim is to create new employment opportunities and improve the environment of those areas. Within 'designated districts' the local authorities concerned have powers to make loans at commercial rates of up to 90 per cent of the value of land and buildings, for land purchase and works such as construction, modification of buildings and installation of services. They also have powers to declare 'industrial improvement areas' (IIAs) and make grants and loans within them for environmental improvements. In addition, local authorities in partnership areas (see page 26) can make loans which are interest-free for up to two years for site-works and access roads; they can also make grants to assist with the rent of commercial and industrial buildings and to help small firms. Since there are many vacant or disused sites in these areas, loans can also be made for site preparation works, the aim being to compensate for the extra costs of using these rather than green-field

sites. All this is designed to give the local authorities concerned the means to take positive action in revitalising the inner areas.

Local authority initiatives designed to improve the lot of the town and city dweller are not of course confined to actions aimed at employment. The examples already quoted in this Report show how varied they can be. For example there are the selective and patient policies of gradual renewal applied in the Jericho district in Oxford (page 63); the help with environmental grants, landscaping and traffic management measures in the Woodlands area in Glasgow (page 81); the provision of mortgages and legal and other assistance in the general improvement area in Macclesfield (page 57); and the activities of the local authority in the lower Swansea Valley (page 42) and in Covent Garden (page 88). These are only a few of the countless examples that could be provided by local authorities throughout the country.

Neither should actions directed at improving leisure and recreational activities be overlooked. These can range from the provision of large leisure centres catering for many sporting activities and with many thousands of users each week, to small adventure playgrounds for children. There are also such ventures as the 'one o'clock clubs' set up by the Parks department of the Greater London Council, which entail an area in a park being set aside between 1 p.m. and 5 p.m. each weekday where trained staff look after children under the age of five, leaving parents free to roam around the rest of the park.

All these are simply random examples of the many-sided nature of urban management. If in future urban renewal proceeds with a more judicious balance between redevelopment, conservation and rehabilitation, and on a smaller scale and at a slower pace, the role of the local authorities as urban managers will become even more important. They will be increasingly involved in harnessing and stimulating renewal activities by a wide range of bodies. The inner area partnerships are deepening their experience of working in partnership with central government, industry, trade unions, and numerous other private bodies interested in various facets of the inner area problem. Within local authorities the process demands the closest possible co-ordination and integration of the policies and actions of many separate departments. Within central government an 'inner area dimension' has been added to national investment programmes controlled by several different Departments in which national priorities and investment constraints may otherwise have pulled in different directions. This is an interesting development which could have significant implications for the future.

7

Planning in the future

Some lessons

There are several lessons to be learned from British urban planning experience since the end of the war.

First, a firm and comprehensive system controlling the use and development of all land is an important prerequisite for any urban planning policy. In the United Kingdom this is effected by the development control system instituted in the Town and Country Planning Act of 1947. It has stood the test of time with only minor modifications. It has been of crucial importance in ensuring that the planned, and even larger voluntary movement of people from the conurbations and large cities has been accommodated in suitable locations without extensive spoliation of the countryside.

Secondly, green belts can be successful in containing the peripheral expansion of cities. This requires firm control over development within the green belt areas on a uniform basis throughout the country, and full public support for the concept. In the United Kingdom there is a deep-rooted acceptance of the need for, and value, of green belts. This has ensured their survival despite intense development pressures which arise in towns and villages beyond the green belt.

Thirdly, the new town and town development programmes have shown that it is possible and practicable to plan and build thriving townships—by joint public/private sector efforts—which have not been simply dormitory housing estates. The government-financed new town development corporation has proved an effective instrument in master-minding the long-term development of a town within a clearly defined area. These towns, largely self-contained in employment and offering a pleasant environment, have developed their own roots and character. Who would have predicted in the early days that Harlow in Essex would have become a flourishing centre of voluntary musical activity, or that their football team would prove to be 'giant-killers' in a recent Football Association cup competition. Most of the new towns are now thriving communities as the third generation grows up. Some of course have suffered the vicissitudes of economic change as firms close down in periods of recession, as happens to all towns, old and new.

Fourthly, it has proved possible to accommodate more traffic within the existing urban road framework than was originally envisaged and without the dire consequences predicted. The strong climate of opinion against large-scale urban motorways has stimulated effective and at times complicated methods of traffic management, including computerised control of traffic in London and other cities, such as Nottingham. Traffic thrombosis has been averted, though whether permanently or merely temporarily remains to be seen. It has also been possible to free many town centres of traffic, a step which despite early misgivings has proved to be economically successful as well as environmentally more pleasant.

Fifth, comprehensive urban redevelopment can be too massive and too fast; it then becomes physically and socially disruptive and unacceptable. This is what happened in the United Kingdom in the 1950s and early 1960s. Much urban redevelopment was certainly necessary, given the national housing shortage and the daunting legacy of slums inherited from the Industrial Revolution. But large-scale 'clear felling' of slum areas and other extensive areas in and around town centres in the interests of urgent and speedy urban renewal has produced many problems. Too little attention was given at the time to the existence of cheap, if sub-standard, housing near town centres, which provided a useful source of accommodation for low-income groups. These areas of overcrowded housing set in a drab, depressing environment were obvious targets for comprehensive redevelopment, but the destruction of the close-knit community life which had flourished there was overlooked, or at least the difficulties of recreating it in the redeveloped areas was greatly underestimated. Since private-enterprise housing tended to be concentrated in the suburbs and on green-field sites, the slum areas became the domain of high-density rented accommodation owned by local authorities, and the variety of housing available in these areas was correspondingly reduced. Too little attention was paid to the fact that rapid change of familiar surroundings affects most of the more vulnerable members of society. Small firms interspersed with slum housing were swept away, and small businesses operating in run-down and shabby back-street premises on the edge of town centres either were rehoused (at higher rents) in more clinically modern premises or simply vanished. A less frenetic pace in redevelopment and less reliance on the bulldozer might well have mitigated many of these problems.

Sixth, if urban redevelopment destroys character and variety in the urban townscape, strenuous efforts should be made to ensure new variety in the new development replacing the old. In the new towns considerable efforts were made to introduce variety—in house designs, house types, in housing layouts, housing tenures, in the layouts of industrial estates and in shopping centres. At times these efforts may have been rather too self-conscious, but in the main these experiments in new urbanisation have developed into thriving and still growing communities.

In existing towns, the wave of reconstruction which marked the 1950s and 1960s has proved less successful in bringing new variety and richness to the urban environment. Many of the old town centres had considerable character, reflecting the individual nature of the town itself. They were of course becoming increasingly traffic-congested and inefficient, while the new town centres, with their supermarkets and traffic-free, air-conditioned shopping precincts, are undoubtedly more efficient and pleasant to shop in. But the latter are often uniform and cosmopolitan in their design, and have failed to retain the local character and style. Elsewhere, the rich diversity of the older residential areas has been replaced by high-density blocks of flats.

Finally, the various elements of urban renewal—redevelopment, rehabilitation and conservation—need to be carefully balanced if they are to mirror the natural and ceaseless forces of change which have always operated in towns and cities throughout history. British urban planning policies have been somewhat unbalanced in this respect. In retrospect it is now clear that there was too much emphasis on massive and speedy redevelopment, with too little emphasis on renovation and conservation, in the 1950s and 1960s. The redevelopment policy was natural and acceptable in the climate of opinion at that time. Indeed in a wider historical perspective it was simply continuing the emphasis on new and rapid development which had lasted for 150 years since the dawn of the Industrial Revolution and which had continued unabated throughout the 20th century. Now it is found wanting because of its effects and consequences. The reaction to those consequences has been a move towards comprehensive renovation and comprehensive conservation. This in turn may be judged in the future to have been too unbalanced, with too little emphasis on the scope for sensitive redevelopment. By the end of the 1970s the work on the problems of the inner areas had stimulated a clearer recognition of the complex inter-relationships between the physical, social and economic environments in urban areas and the need to integrate and develop comprehensive town-planning, social and economic policies if the requisite solutions were to be found. There was also a growing awareness that a more balanced form of urban renewal might be more appropriate—slower, small-scale and diverse and more responsive to local needs and wishes—in short, gradual renewal.

Looking ahead – technological changes

Looking ahead to the 1980s, it is tempting to predict that British urban policies will be dominated by the problems of the inner city areas, while elsewhere the emphasis will be on a more balanced form of urban renewal which blends conservation, renovation and redevelopment in a careful and sensitive manner, working on a small scale and at a much slower pace than in the past. This would be a natural evolutionary development in the light of post-war experience. The question arises, however, whether policies designed to resolve the specific problems of the 1960s and 1970s will be appropriate for the problems of the 1980s.

The 1980s are shrouded in more uncertainty than usual. It could be argued that the Western European nations have been adjusting to rapid change for well over 150 years, and the Victorians would certainly have asserted with every justification that they were living in such a period. Even so there are signs that we are now moving into a period of accelerating change triggered by the energy crises, the microprocessor revolution, and the developments taking place in information technology, materials technology and biotechnology.

The first OPEC oil crisis in 1973 may well prove to have been the watershed in the development of energy technologies. The latest assessment is that fuels other than oil will have to meet increases in world energy demand after the mid-1980s. In addition they will also have to compensate for a slowly falling oil supply. It is likely to become increasingly important to preserve oil supplies as raw materials for the petro-chemical industry and for certain forms of transport. Energy conservation and the development of alternative energy sources could become a new national imperative, and energy conservation could well be a dominant feature in future urban policies.

Exhaustion of natural resources, other than oil and natural gas, is not considered likely to be a serious world problem in the next 10 to 15 years but it could become a constraint on industrial activity in the longer term. This is already stimulating developments in materials technology, such as the substitution of cheaper raw materials, their recycling, and greater economy in their use in manufacturing. It is also stimulating computer-aided design and manufacture, and developments in biotechnology (i.e. the exploitation of renewable, biological resources instead of non-renewable, mineral resources) as a possible future basis for industrial technology.

Some future problems

Then there are the rapid developments in microelectronics—the widespread adoption of the microchip, with its potential effects on employment both in the destruction of jobs and the creation of new ones. Within the microelectronics field the subject of information technology is becoming increasingly important. There is a growing need for fast and efficient means of communication, and tele-communication, tele-conferencing, word processors, etc., are likely to have a deep impact on office procedures, organisation and design.

Add to the complex interactions of all these emerging technologies other social changes— the great expansion of leisure activities, the spread of do-it-yourself activities and changes in traditional family patterns, and it is clear that the 1980s will be a decade of great uncertainty. Prediction is always hazardous; in the present circumstances it is more than usually so. But some attempt needs to be made to assess future trends and problems so that future urban planning policies may be shaped accordingly.

An increasingly stringent policy of energy conservation could well have pervasive long-term effects on urban policies. The coming of the motor car and an era of cheap energy facilitated an exodus of people from the large cities. Will energy shortages, and the increasing cost of travel whether by car or public transport, reverse this trend? Will journeys to work shorten and more compact urban structures develop? Will this trend help to arrest the decline of the big cities and possibly prove to be the trigger for effective renewal of the inner city areas?

On the other hand will the communications revolution, with its prospects of mini-computer terminals in the home, increase the pressures for dispersal, undermine the *raison d'être* of large office blocks in city centres and affect future shopping habits? If the home becomes more of a work-place, will do-it-yourself activities and personal leisure activities centred on the home also reinforce dispersal trends, creating a demand for housing at lower densities with enough space to pursue gardening and other hobbies?

Alternatively, these contradictory trends could combine to produce a situation where there is some movement back into the cities to save travelling costs, but only if high-density development is replaced by medium-density, low-rise schemes offering opportunities for personal hobby and work activities. In this case we could expect to see the development of a less dense urban pattern with more facilities for gardens and allotments, which would of course place corresponding expansionary pressures on encircling green belts. Planning policies will need to be extremely flexible to embrace some of these possibilities.

Energy conservation has other implications for urban planning. For example, district heating schemes using heat from power stations could become more widespread. There is an interesting experiment in the Byker housing area in Newcastle which re-cycles domestic waste back into residential heating for the area. To become economic such schemes might require high-density development which conflicts with some of the other possibilities mentioned above.

Energy conservation could have profound effects on house design. There is already active discussion about housing which is 'low-energy, loose-fit and long-life'—i.e. which conserves energy and is readily adaptable internally to meet changing family needs, yet sufficiently durable externally to last for a long time. If solar energy becomes economic, what are the environmental implications of buildings with solar panels in, say, conservation areas? What standards are to be adopted for the better insulation of existing housing and other buildings in the interests of energy conservation? Questions of cost and the degree to which such measures should be made compulsory also arise.

Shopping habits and retail patterns could well change if shopping by car becomes less attractive because of rising petrol costs, and if the entry of cars into city centres is increasingly controlled through parking restrictions and other measures. Ordering goods via a home-based computer terminal is also on the horizon. The small shop offering a local and personal service may become attractive again. This would parallel the present emphasis on the value of small firms as providers of employment at a time when employment structures are changing rapidly and because of their inherent adaptability to change.

The development control system is also under conflicting pressures. On the one hand there is concern over the economic costs of delays in dealing with planning applications and a consciousness of the need to speed up and streamline procedures. On the other hand there is concern about the adequacy of the public inquiry system as a means of effectively exploring the policies underlying a specific proposal—for example the whole policy for motorway construction or for nuclear energy. Reconciling conflicting pressures for greater public involvement in planning decisions with greater responsiveness to change has never been easy; it is likely to be even more difficult in a period of accelerating change coupled with emphasis on local participation.

It could be argued that the pace and complexity of the technological changes looming ahead are so great and so profound that post-war experience has become largely irrelevant; policies should be thought out anew. But such an argument underestimates the sheer durability of our urban structure. Towns and cities do not change dramatically overnight. They are likely to be recognisably the same in the 1990s as they are today, hopefully with a generally better urban environment. If the forthcoming technological changes are accepted as opportunities rather than as threats to the established order, their effects are likely to be absorbed into future urban life in ways at present only dimly foreseen.

Gradual renewal

A broad policy of gradual renewal may prove to be the most appropriate approach to these uncertainties. Gradual renewal is essentially small-scale, unobtrusive, incremental and continuous. It means working with the 'grain' of the urban fabric in an undramatic manner and to long time-scales. It is a process in tune with the natural, age-long processes of change which, before the frenetic activity of the Industrial Revolution, helped to produce the interesting variety and pleasing townscapes of English towns and villages.

This approach has been evolving on several fronts in the last few years. It is already a feature of housing policies, as described in chapter 3, and it is apparent in transport policies with their emphasis on traffic restraint, the greater use of public transport and small-scale, incremental urban road schemes. It coincides with the trends in public participation—towards more active involvement in public authority planning, self-help schemes, tenants' involvement in the management of local authority housing estates, and community schemes and local enterprise trusts in inner areas. It matches the aspirations and activities of hundreds of local amenity societies operating throughout the land, and it fits the current public mood of hostility to dramatic changes of well-known environments. It allows local diversity and presents a challenging role of urban 'managership' to the local authorities. Compared with comprehensive redevelopment it is less costly to operate—a factor not to be overlooked in the period of limited resources foreseeable in the 1980s.

But this concept of gradual or natural renewal of urban areas is deceptively simple. It may well turn out to be a sophisticated and demanding approach. It could easily degenerate into *ad hoc*, piecemeal and unplanned changes which cumulatively do little to improve the quality of urban life.

There are several difficulties and problems inherent in the concept which will need to be resolved. How are the natural forces of urban change to be guided and effectively harnessed? Is it possible for a local authority to have a clear and consistent strategy or vision for the long-term renewal of an urban area without resort to a guiding framework? Detailed plans could well be too inflexible and too cumbersome an instrument for a fine-tuned renewal policy. Developers need some clarity and certainty in local plans if they are to proceed with confidence in their activities, and plans that are too broad-brushed can be unhelpful to them. But plans that are too detailed can stifle local initiatives. Will gradual renewal perhaps require informal local 'community plans' in those areas where the inhabitants have both the interest and the will to participate in urban renewal? If so, should they cover social and other policies, and how will they be fitted into the larger statutory development plan system, or will this system itself need to be reappraised?

There could be implications for the various standards which govern so many aspects of urban activities. Is it necessary to apply uniform and rigid standards relating to planning, byelaws, noise, cost, etc., to every conceivable aspect of a multi-faceted process of gradual renewal? Housing renovation has already encountered the problem that uniform application of a high standard of improvement to all houses in a general improvement area, or a housing action area, can be uneconomic and involve an unacceptable degree of compulsion. Where house improvement is tailored to individual wishes and capacity to pay, the result is often a variety of standards ranging from a basic minimum to a high level of improvement, as was demonstrated in the Oxford example described in chapter 3.

There are obvious difficulties in relaxing, or applying flexibly, standards which affect human life and safety. But some standards may need to be realistically reviewed. There is a natural tendency to 'play safe' in formulating general standards, especially when this is done in response to a public outcry over some disaster. There may be less difficulty about applying more flexible standards in the field of planning control—densities, plot ratios, height controls, external design etc. Each application for planning permission can at least be considered on its merits within the broad framework of the particular town plan in force at the time. But even here there are problems: there are always complaints if standards are not administered with scrupulous fairness. The pressures to apply high standards on a rigidly uniform and even-handed basis are intense. Yet the cumulative effect of all these standards, each impeccable when viewed in isolation, may well be to inhibit the diversity inherent in gradual renewal, minimising the difference in actions and results which can emerge not only between towns but also between different areas within the same town. There are difficult issues here. Current proposals to relax fiscal and other policies and controls to stimulate development in 'local enterprise zones' in inner city areas could have implications in the wider field of renewal.

Then there is the long time-scale implicit in the gradual approach to renewal. Unless there are strong pressures for rapid change, the whole process implies small-scale changes made as and when opportunities arise. It is slow and undramatic. To this extent it may be incompatible with the much shorter time-scales imposed by the electoral needs of local and central government, unless the broad approach commands general, all-party consent. It was precisely this kind of consensus which underpinned the successful construction of the new towns over a period of nearly a quarter of a century. Gradual renewal will need a similar consensus. It is not a simple policy or an easy option.

Nevertheless, a policy of gradual renewal, in which redevelopment, conservation and renovation are carefully balanced, may prove to be the most appropriate in a period of great change and uncertainty, despite the problems inherent in this approach. Large-scale, grandiose plans designed to make rapid and major changes to the urban environment on predetermined lines, and to a predetermined time-scale, could be totally inappropriate in such a period. Experience in the 1960s shows how quickly such plans can become outdated and irrelevant to events. At the same time, excessive preservation of the *status quo* and resistance to change (as distinct from the more creative forms of conservation) could be equally inappropriate and stultifying in the face of the sustained pressures for change which are inevitable.

Gradual renewal may not be an easy option, nevertheless its small-scale, incremental and pragmatic nature does give it great flexibility to meet changing circumstances. Properly developed, it could produce a rich diversity of local responses in towns and cities, rooted in local needs and wishes. This could not but help to induce a greater awareness of the urban environment and also possibly recreate some of the local community spirit lost through indiscriminate redevelopment.

Moreover the fostering of community spirit is one of the keynotes in any campaign for urban renaissance. For decades people have voted with their feet and left the larger cities in search of a better environment. Preserving the *status quo* in those cities will not attract them back. There is no simple or single answer. Instead, a variety of policies needs to be considered. A determined onslaught on the physical, social and economic problems of the inner areas must go hand in hand with small-scale, sensitive and sophisticated renewal of other areas in response to pressures for change and local needs. A sustained assault on urban pollution in all its forms must not divert attention from the need for more diversity in the density, quality and variety of housing available. Diversity of employment opportunities needs to be matched by a greater diversity of leisure opportunities within urban areas. All these measures in concert would at least go some way to halting the continued decline of our towns and cities.

Bibliography

Administrative Tribunals and Inquiries,
Committee on,
Report (Franks Report), Cmnd 218.
v+115 pp, HMSO, 1957.

Advisory Council for Applied Research and
Development,
*Technological change : threats and opportunities
for the United Kingdom.*
38 pp, HMSO, 1979.

Bor, Walter,
The making of cities.
xiii+256 pp, Leonard Hill, 1972.

Buchanan, Colin Douglas,
The state of Britain.
87 pp, Faber, 1972.
The text of the Chichele Lectures 1972.

Burns, Wilfred,
*New towns for old : the technique for urban
renewal.*
xii+226 pp, Leonard Hill, 1963.

Central Office of Information,
Reference Division,
Environmental planning in Britain
(Reference Pamphlet 9).
65 pp, HMSO, 1979.

Cherry, Gordon E.,
*Urban change and planning : a history of urban
development in Britain since 1750.*
ix+227 pp, G. T. Foulis, 1972.

Civic Trust,
*Urban wasteland : a report on land lying
dormant in cities, towns and villages in Britain*
(written and compiled by Timothy Cantell).
56 pp, The Civic Trust, 1977.

Civic Trust,
The local amenity movement
(by Anthony Barker).
36 pp, The Civic Trust, 1976.
Issued as a contribution to the United
Nations Conference on Human Settlements,
Vancouver, 1976.

Cullingworth, J. B.,
Environmental planning, Vol 1,
'Reconstruction and land use planning
1939–47' (Peacetime History Series).
x+283 pp, HMSO, 1975.

Cullingworth, J. B.,
Environmental planning, Vol 3, 'New towns
policy' (Peacetime History Series).
xvii+629 pp, HMSO, 1979.

Cullingworth, J. B.,
Problems of an urban society, Vol II, 'The
social content of planning' (Birmingham
University Centre for Urban and Regional
Studies, Urban and Regional Studies No. 5).
191 pp, Allen and Unwin, 1973.

Cullingworth, J. B.,
Town and country planning in Britain.
287 pp, 6th ed, Allen and Unwin, 1976.

Department of the Environment,
*Change or decay : final report of the Liverpool
Inner Area Study*
(Consultants : Hugh Wilson and Lewis
Womersley, Chartered Architects and Town
Planners, in association with Roger Tym and
Associates, Urban and Land Economists,
and Jamieson Mackay and Partners,
Consulting Civil and Transportation
Engineers).
xiv+240 pp, HMSO, 1977.

Department of the Environment,
Clean air today.
vi+38 pp, HMSO, 1974.

Department of the Environment,
English house condition survey 1976/DOE,
Part 1, 'Report of the physical condition
survey' (DOE Housing survey report No. 10).
v+30 pp, HMSO, 1978.

Department of the Environment,
English house condition survey/DOE, Part 2,
'Report of the social survey' (by Barbara E. I.
Bird and Alan O'Dell of the Building
Research Establishment Urban Planning
Division; DOE Housing survey report No. 11)
vi+72 pp, HMSO, 1979.

Department of the Environment,
Housing policy/DOE, Cmnd 6851.
2 vols in 4 (vi+154, v+244, v+160,
iv+210 pp), HMSO, 1977.

Department of the Environment,
*Inner London : policies for dispersal and
balance ; final report of the Lambeth Inner
Area Study,*
(Consultants : Shankland Cox Partnership in
association with the Institute of Community
Studies).
x+243 pp, HMSO, 1977.

Department of the Environment,
*Leisure and the quality of life : a report on
four local experiments,* Vol 1.
x+142 pp, HMSO, 1977.

Department of the Environment,
Planning in the United Kingdom (national
report prepared for Habitat, United Nations
Conference on Human Settlements,
Vancouver, 1976).
124 pp, Department of the Environment, 1976.

Department of the Environment,
Policy for the inner cities, Cmnd 6845.
32 pp, HMSO, 1977.
Issued jointly with the Scottish Office and
the Welsh Office.

Department of the Environment,
*Review of the development control system :
final report* (Chairman: George Dobry, QC).
viii + 238 pp, HMSO, 1975.

Department of the Environment,
Structure plans : the examination in public.
13 pp, Department of the Environment, 1973.
Issued jointly with the Welsh Office and the
Central Office of Information.

Department of the Environment,
*Town and country planning : index to
departmental circulars and other relevant
publications as at* 31 *August* 1979.
26 pp, HMSO, 1979.
Issued jointly with the Welsh Office.

Department of the Environment,
*Unequal city : final report of the Birmingham
Inner Area Study*
Consultants: Llewelyn-Davies, Weeks,
Forestier-Walker and Bor).
xii + 339 pp, HMSO, 1977.

Department of the Environment,
*United Kingdom monograph on current trends
and policies in the fields of housing, building
and planning.*
26 pp, Department of the Environment, 1980.

Department of the Environment,
*What is our heritage? United Kingdom
achievements for European Architectural
Heritage Year* 1975.
xii + 135 pp, HMSO, 1975.

Department of the Environment,
Inner Cities Directorate,
*Industry in the inner cities : a case study in
mixed use development.*
39 pp, Department of the Environment, 1978.

Department of the Environment,
Urban Motorways Committee,
*Report of the Urban Motorways Project Team
to the . . . Committee.*
xi + 287 pp, HMSO, 1973.

Donnison, David, with Soto, Paul,
*The good city—a study of urban development
and policy in Britain*
xi + 221 pp, Heinemann, 1980.

Environmental Board,
Infill development,
iv + 15 pp, HMSO, 1979.

Essex County Council,
County Planning Department,
A design guide for residential areas.
134 pp, Essex County Council, 1973.

Hall, Peter,
Urban and regional planning.
xvii + 312 pp, Penguin Books, 1974.

Hall, Peter, and others,
The containment of urban England
(by Peter Hall, Harry Gracey, Roy Drewett,
and Ray Thomas assisted by Bob Peacock,
Anne Whalley, Chris Smith, Anthony Beck
and Werner Heidmann).
2 vols in 1 vol, 1,112 pp; new ed, Allen and
Unwin, 1977.

Heap, Sir Desmond,
An outline of planning law.
lix + 344 pp, 7th ed, Sweet and Maxwell, 1978.

Jones, Colin,
Urban deprivation and the inner city.
218 pp, Croom Helm, 1979.

Kirby, D. A.,
*Slum housing and residential renewal : the case
in urban Britain.*
xi + 102 pp, Longman, 1979.

Lansley, Stewart,
Housing and public policy.
246 pp, Croom Helm, 1979.

McKay, David H., and Cox, Andrew W.,
The politics of urban change.
297 pp, Croom Helm, 1979.

Matthew, Robert, Johnson-Marshall and
Partners/Department of the Environment,
New life in old towns (report on two pilot
studies on urban renewal in Nelson and
Rawtenstall Municipal Boroughs).
iv + 212 pp, HMSO, 1971.

Ministry of Housing and Local Government,
*The Deeplish study : improvement possibilities
in a district of Rochdale.*
x + 74 pp, HMSO, 1966.

Ministry of Housing and Local Government,
The green belts.
iv + 30 pp, HMSO, 1962.

Ministry of Housing and Local Government,
Old houses into new homes, Cmnd 3602.
29 pp, HMSO, 1968.
Issued jointly with the Welsh Office.

Ministry of Housing and Local Government,
Trees in town and city.
vi + 83 pp, HMSO, 1958.

Ministry of Housing and Local Government,
Committee on Public Participation in
Planning,
People and planning ; report of the committee . . .
(Chairman: A. M. Skeffington).
71 pp, HMSO, 1969.
Issued jointly with the Scottish Development
Department and the Welsh Office.

Ministry of Housing and Local Government,
Planning Advisory Group,
The future of development plans : a report
(Chairman : I. V. Pugh).
v +62 +6 pp, HMSO, 1965.
Joint publication with the Ministry of
Transport and the Scottish Development
Department.

Ministry of Transport,
*Traffic in towns : a study of the long term
problems of traffic in urban areas*
(reports of the Steering Group, Chairman :
Sir Geoffrey Crowther, and the Working
Group, Chairman : Colin Buchanan).
xii +224 pp, HMSO, 1963.

Traffic in towns.
Abridged ed, 263 pp, Penguin, 1963.

Noise Advisory Council,
*The Darlington quiet town experiment,
report by a working group of the . . . Council.*
HMSO, to be published 1980.

Office of the Lord President of the Council,
Committee on the Problem of Noise,
Noise : final report (Chairman : Sir Alan
Wilson), Cmnd 2056.
xii +235 pp, HMSO, 1963.

Organisation for Economic Co-operation
and Development,
For better urban living.
108 pp, Paris, OECD, 1978.

Paris, Chris, and Blackaby, Bob,
*Not much improvement : urban renewal policy
in Birmingham.*
xii +208 pp, Heinemann, 1979.

Roberts, J. Trevor,
General Improvement Areas.
viii +188 pp, Saxon House, 1976.

Royal Town Planning Institute,
*The urban crisis : economic problems and
planning . . .*
(report of proceedings of a seminar held at
the Park Hotel, Cardiff on 12 February 1975;
edited by South Glamorgan County Planning
Department).
78 pp, Royal Town Planning Institute, 1975.

Royal Town Planning Institute,
*The urban crisis : leisure in the urban
environment.*
ii +64 pp, Royal Town Planning
Institute, 1976.

Royal Town Planning Institute,
*The urban crisis, social problems and
planning . . .*
(proceedings of a seminar held at the
University of Strathclyde on 20 November
1974; edited by Janet Brand and Margaret
Cox).
ii +82 pp, Royal Town Planning
Institute, 1975.

Shankland, Graeme,
*Renewing Europe's inner cities : a study
produced for the Council of Europe.*
i +245 pp. Council of Europe, 1978.

Smith, David L.,
Amenity and urban planning.
iv +198 pp, Crosby Lockwood Staples, 1974.

Town and Country Planning Association,
Inner cities of tomorrow
(policy statement).
22 pp, Town and Country Planning
Association, 1977.

United Nations Conference on Human
Settlements, Vancouver, 1976,
Report of Habitat (held 31 May—11 June
1976).
iv +183 pp, New York, United Nations, 1976.

Wilcox, David and Richards, David,
London : the heartless city.
172 pp, Thames Television, 1977.

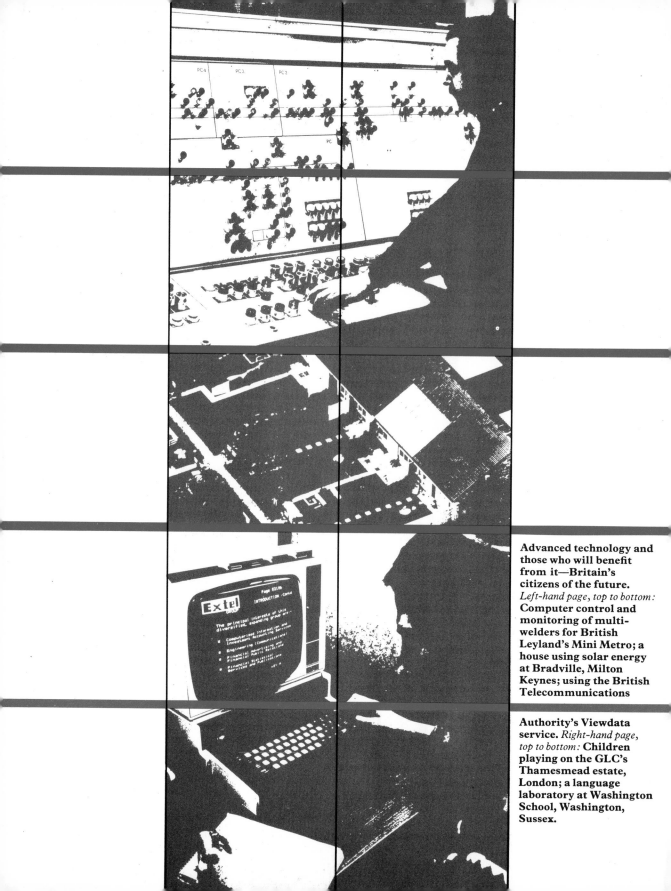

Advanced technology and those who will benefit from it—Britain's citizens of the future. *Left-hand page, top to bottom:* Computer control and monitoring of multi-welders for British Leyland's Mini Metro; a house using solar energy at Bradville, Milton Keynes; using the British Telecommunications Authority's Viewdata service. *Right-hand page, top to bottom:* Children playing on the GLC's Thamesmead estate, London; a language laboratory at Washington School, Washington, Sussex.